SKILLS & VALUES:
ADMINISTRATIVE LAW

Skills & Values:
Administrative Law

Alfred C. Aman, Jr.
Indiana University
Maurer School of Law

William Penniman
Of Counsel
Sutherland, Asbill & Brennan
Washington, D.C.

9781422483282

Library of Congress Cataloging-in-Publication Data
Aman, Alfred C.
Administrative law / Alfred C. Aman, Jr., William Penniman.
p. cm. -- (Skills & values)
ISBN 978-1-4224-8328-2
1. Administrative law--United States. 2. Administrative procedure--United States. 3. Administrative courts--United States. I. Penniman, William. II. Title.
KF5402.A84 2012
342.73'06--dc23
2012014997

This publication is designed to provide authoritative information in regard to the subject matter covered. It is sold with the understanding that the publisher is not engaged in rendering legal, accounting, or other professional services. If legal advice or other expert assistance is required, the services of a competent professional should be sought.

LexisNexis and the Knowledge Burst logo are registered trademarks of Reed Elsevier Properties Inc., used under license. Matthew Bender and the Matthew Bender Flame Design are registered trademarks of Matthew Bender Properties Inc.

> NOTE TO USERS
> To ensure that you are using the latest materials available in this area, please be sure to periodically check the LexisNexis Law School web site for downloadable updates and supplements at www.lexisnexis.com/lawschool.

Editorial Offices
121 Chanlon Rd., New Providence, NJ 07974 (908) 464-6800
201 Mission St., San Francisco, CA 94105-1831 (415) 908-3200
www.lexisnexis.com

MATTHEW◆BENDER

(2012–Pub.3321)

ACKNOWLEDGEMENTS

Alfred Aman

Would like to acknowledge Anne Fishbeck, IU Law, '13, John Fleming, IU Law, '12, Jennifer Hepp, IU Law, '13, Melanie Jesteadt, IU Law, '13, Jessica Vizvary, IU Law, '13, and Jacob Wood, IU Law, '13.

William Penniman

Would like to acknowledge David Moody, Bee Bentley and Paul Forshay of Sutherland, Asbill & Brennan for their assistance.

INTRODUCTION

This book sets out to teach administrative law by using an organization that starts each Part with an overview — then goes to specific chapters which explore particular topics important in administrative law practice. Part I is administrative adjudication, Part II is agency rulemaking, Part III is judicial review, Part Four is Information, and Part Five is New and Multiple issues. Each short overview tries to help situate the exercises that follow into the appropriate section of a traditional administrative law course. They also are intended to help anchor these exercises in a particular part of the course if the book is used as the primary text. This book also has an online component, where additional materials, statutes, and information are available on the **LEXISNEXIS WEBCOURSE**.

Each exercise indicates a time for completion, indicated by the below icon, each representing 15 minutes.

As well as a level of difficulty, represented by 1 — 5 "black diamonds," as shown below.

LEARNING OBJECTIVES

- Persuading an administrative law agency;
- Basic questions to consider when facing an administrative law issue;
- How to advise and work with clients in an administrative law context;
- Finding the applicable agency rules and orders;
- Preparing a motion to intervene and protest; requesting hearings;
- How to deal with potential intervenors;
- How to recommend appropriate procedures; dealing with settlements;
- Designing and drafting a settlement proposal;
- How to find rulemaking proceedings and file comments;
- Developing a rulemaking strategy;
- Dealing with ethical issues;
- Drafting petitions for reviews;
- Drafting briefs;
- Challenging existing rules;
- Preparing a FOIA request;
- Getting guidance from an administrative agency;
- Dealing with informal agency action; and
- Dealing with privatization, outsourcing agency responsibilities.

Table of Contents

Table of Contents

Table of Contents

INTRODUCTION

Practicing Administrative Law

Practicing administrative law requires a lawyer to draw upon nearly all the skills he or she is expected to have. These include legal analysis, policy analysis, compliance counseling, trial and appellate litigation, negotiation, contract drafting, regulation drafting, and lobbying. A broad view of issues, judgment, creativity and a good sense of strategy are vital to effectively practicing administrative law.

Approaching an administrative law question is similar, in many ways, to approaching any legal issue. You need to understand your client's problem, the solution it seeks, the legal and procedural frameworks applicable to the problem, and the forum where the issue will be resolved.

There are important differences, however, between practicing administrative law and other areas of practice.

For one thing, the ranges of potentially relevant issues and decision makers are often wider than in a typical legal context. A contract dispute, for example, will typically involve two contracting parties; the terms of their agreement and their disagreement over those terms; application of general principles of contract law (often common law) to the facts you can discover; rules of civil procedure; and a court or arbitrator who will need to be persuaded if you do not reach a settlement. In addition to the law, you need to understand the elements of the dispute, the contracting parties' expectations (then and now), the words of the agreement and the parties' inclinations to pursue a dispute; and, you need a strategy for persuading the other side to yield or compromise or for persuading a decision maker of the merits of your case.

Similarly, a typical tort action will involve factual questions of who did what to whom; evaluation of the nature and extent of the harms; application of established legal principles to determine liability for such actions; and procedural questions about how to obtain the relevant facts, how to present them to a decision maker and how to get a decision. In both types of cases, you will need strategies for discovery and for persuasion to achieve your client's best outcome.

Administrative law, on the other hand, generally involves government regulation of private activities in order to achieve a public benefit, such as mitigating environmental or economic harms to bystanders. It generally involves broader issues than a simple two-party dispute (though a two-party dispute may be the context of the legal dispute presented by your client). Even when an agency is "prosecuting" a particular company, as when the Federal Trade Commission is pursuing an antitrust or unfair practices case against an individual company, the backdrop of public policy looms large. Third parties may wish to intervene in your client's matter in order to comment on the impacts the agency's choices could have on them or on the public generally.

Not surprisingly, the legal and regulatory policy puzzle can be very complex; and policy choices can be fluid. An agency needs always to be sensitive to "what if" questions about the collateral consequences of its actions — which means outside lawyers need to anticipate those questions as well. These impact questions can invoke wide-ranging arguments about economics, incentives/disincentives, environmental impacts, health consequences, financial impacts to particular entities, and perceptions of just administration of laws, to name a few.

In the administrative law context, you also need to consider the possibility that multiple government agencies may have a stake in a given set of issues, and may be applying different laws and regulations to similar or overlapping issues. Sometimes, agencies file formal comments in other agencies' proceedings. Other times, agencies may consult behind the scenes. Influencing those other agencies may help your client achieve its objectives before the lead agency.

Furthermore, interconnected regulatory issues may arise at the federal, state, and local levels. State and local agencies may have very different views from federal regulators, and, if they cannot persuade the federal agency to do their bidding, they may try to limit a federal ruling's impact within a state. Issues of federal preemption can easily arise.

In addition to generally applicable procedural statutes, like the Administrative Procedure Act, each agency will be governed by substantive statutes which define its powers and jurisdiction, the policies it is to implement, and, in many cases, specific procedural requirements which supersede general statutes, like the APA. Beyond the applicable statutes, each agency with jurisdiction over a piece of the puzzle will likely have its own regulations and a body of decisional precedent which you will need to investigate. Judicial decisions reviewing agency actions will place boundaries on the policies and practices implemented by the agency.

Each agency will have its own rules of procedure and, in some cases, own cultures for dealing with the public and for deciding issues brought before it. Procedures for judicial review may vary from one agency and one statute to another.

Perhaps most important, you need to understand the policies the relevant agencies are trying to implement. Agencies are required to implement statutes to achieve public policy goals which are larger than your client's individual interest. Sometimes, the statutes' requirements are clear, and the agency is needed simply to administer the clear requirements. More often, agencies are expected to take a statute's general policies and apply them in a variety of circumstances, which the legislators could not possibly have catalogued and distinguished. The agencies are expected to develop and adapt those policies as circumstances change over time. Regulatory statutes often contain very general principles, such as those requiring an agency to approve rates that are "just and reasonable," or to approve facilities and services that are "required by the public interest," or to require an industry to implement the "best available technology" for pollution control. Even if a statute clearly identifies a policy objective, an evolving industry may require constantly evolving standards, which could not possibly be written into a statute.

Statutes commit important policy issues to administrative agencies, rather than courts, because agency bureaucracies are needed to administer regulatory statutes on a day-to-day basis, and they are more capable than courts of developing deep expertise in the industries and subject matter they oversee. Such expertise is critical to achieving legislators' policy goals. Also, unlike courts, which are expected to rule only on specific issues raised by specific litigants, administrative agencies are expected to initiate regulatory actions, not just to respond to complaints or proposals by others. They must routinely oversee and investigate matters within their jurisdiction, actively enforce their existing regulations, and initiate proposals to improve their regulatory rules and practices.

In practice, much of an agency's expertise is found in its professional staff. Politically appointed heads of agencies may have training or experience well-suited to the agency or they may have little relevant expertise when they arrive, hopefully learning on the job with the assistance of the staff and thoughtful submissions in proceedings. These ultimate decision makers rely heavily on their staff for support, guidance and implementation.

Herein lies one of the most important differences between practicing administrative law and traditional judicial litigation. Unlike judicial litigation, administrative decisions are the products of multi-faceted agencies with a professional staff — *i.e.*, bureaucracies. In civil or criminal litigation, both the record and the decision makers are clearly visible to the litigants. Although some administrative adjudications are conducted before an administrative law judge ("ALJ") and closely resemble judicial litigation, others are far more complex. Agency decisions are often the product of teams of individuals who provide data, analysis, drafting, policy and legal recommendations to the administrator or commission. The staff contributing to the decision will likely be divided into offices based upon substantive responsibilities (*e.g.*, based on expertise in law, specific industries, particular technologies, environmental or economic impacts, and enforcement techniques), which, in turn, may be divided into areas of expertise (*e.g.*, addressing distinct environmental issues, such as water, air, land, species, mitigation technology, etc.). To those levels of bureaucracy, one must add the personal advisory staff to the administrator or the commissioners who bear ultimate responsibility for an agency's decisions. In addition, an agency may have a trial staff, an investigatory staff, its own solicitor's office (to handle judicial review proceedings), a secretary's office to process and maintain records, and a public relations office. If the agency is headed by a commission, the Chair will be particularly important in setting priorities and overseeing the staff.

A rulemaking proposal will be developed with contributions from each of the relevant offices, and the public's comments will (in theory) be reviewed by each of the offices involved in the process. Even appeals from an administrative law judge may be reviewed by a variety of offices, which will advise the administrator or commissioners on how to deal with appeals. Not surprisingly, each of the offices may develop distinctive views of how to treat a matter, and they may argue among each other over recommended policies and decisions. Depending on the subject matter, one office may take the lead on a matter, but it is safe to say that others will weigh in, and the general counsel's office will always be involved in order to assure the legal defensibility of a potential agency action. The basic content of a rule or order is likely to be largely drafted before it gets to the final decision maker who may, of course, insist upon rewriting all or part of the order. Knowing who is going to be involved and addressing your comments to the different groups' concerns can be very important to getting an outcome favorable to your client.

Persuading an Administrative Agency

In short, when approaching an administrative law problem, you need to understand the regulatory agency's policy mandates, its substantive and procedural means of implementing those policies, and how it works internally. Woodenly reciting an agency's mandate to act in the "public interest" will not get you very far if you do not know how the agency's leaders currently interpret the "public interest" and how they apply that standard in individual cases similar to your client's.

Substantively, you need to develop a strategy for fitting your client's requests and facts within the agency's policy framework. And, if you cannot achieve a very good fit, you need to understand the ultimate policy goals well enough to design a strategy to persuade the agency either to modify its current policy choices or its means of achieving those policy goals. Failing that, you may need to position your client to persuade a court that application of the agency's rules and policies to your client's facts was not consistent with the facts or the relevant statutory policies or the agency's own regulations or precedent.

Despite grousing by some people (possibly your client) about allegedly "lazy" or "out-of-touch bureaucrats," beware of such characterizations. Not only would employing such language offend the people who will decide your client's matter, but the characterizations are generally wrong. Most agency officials are, in fact, very interested in getting their policies right and in correctly applying those policies to the facts before them. Senior staff members likely have many years of experience dealing with the industries they regulate. They want to know the potential impacts of their actions on the "public interest" and how to maximize benefits while minimizing harms. Where relevant, detailed technical advice from commenters is both welcome and potentially influential. Agency officials want to understand the workings of the industries before them, so that solutions are practical and efficient. If they can achieve their regulatory objectives while enhancing (or, at least, not harming) an industry's outlook, they will generally try to do that. Regulators also want to adopt rules and policies that can be applied predictably and consistently. And, not surprisingly, they do not want their decisions to be overturned by a court, nor do they want to be harassed by a legislative committee chairman.

More than in most areas of law, administrative law involves policy disputes and policy persuasion. Judges in civil and criminal proceedings have some room to interpret statutes and common law precedents, but they are generally expected to apply the law as they find it. Administrative agencies are given greater flexibility to create the policies that fill out the law. In developing their regulations and precedent, they want to know the positive and negative public consequences of their proposed agency actions.

Thus, the scope of arguments to an agency can easily bring into play claims about broad public impacts from a particular decision (*e.g., if you disapprove our application, the public will suffer shortages of electricity or if you approve our application cleaner energy sources will displace coal to generate electricity thereby benefiting the public*). Or, the argument may urge a change in regulation by invoking recent changes in industry structure or practices (*e.g., the public interest requires a change in policy because new technology makes the old policy assumptions obsolete or because a change will bring about greater efficiencies or lower costs while still protecting consumers*). Or, you may be able to invoke collateral consequences as justification for your proposed action (*e.g., approval of that project will damage a wildlife sanctuary*).

An agency's policies can be changed if the changes are adequately supported by a factual record and an adequate explanation of the basis for the change.[1] Policies can be formally changed through orders in individual cases, rules, policy statements, and declaratory orders. Thus, proponents of change may have a variety of procedural vehicles to seek change. A party who seeks to change a policy or regulation will need a lawyer who can develop strategies for persuasion and an administrative record to support the changes. Sometimes, those strategies may take years of gradual persuasion to succeed.

On the other hand, administrative policymakers do not have a free hand. Regulatory agencies are creatures of statutes. Boundaries are placed on an agency's actions by the laws they implement, by judicial decisions, by an agency's own rules and precedents, and by its need to compile a supportive record of decision. Further, consistency in applying the terms of a statute is a goal in itself. Thus, while the wording of laws administered by agencies are often flexible and require judgment to administer, they are not wholly elastic.

Judicial review of agency actions (or inaction) provides another array of issues that go beyond a typical two-party law suit. Issues of standing, ripeness, deference, scope of authority, and the reasonableness of agency policies frequently arise in judicial review of administrative actions. These are important questions that involve judicial policies and the constitutional role of the judiciary versus the legislative and executive branches.

Furthermore, because agencies and the statutes they implement are the product of legislative action, legislative oversight and the possibility of legislative action may offer potential avenues for achieving a client's objectives. Since administrative agencies may be part of the executive branch, pressure from higher up in the executive branch or from sister agencies may offer a strategy that may benefit a client (or backfire if agency officials resent the interference). Even independent agencies

---

[1] Creativity must be tempered by realism and history. While some ideas or issues are truly new and can warrant a policy change, an agency implementing a long-standing statutory requirement has likely considered many of the issues you initially think of. Still, even old statutory language can be applied in new ways if new circumstances arise or if new policy thinking is in vogue.

may wish to hear from fellow government agencies about the positive or negative consequences of a particular action they are considering taking. Concerns about *ex parte* contacts need to be considered, but enlisting support from other agencies or the legislature may become a helpful part of your strategy in a particular matter.

In sum, if you find public policy questions more fun than resolving issues of who-hit-whom or who-breached-what, or if you are interested in how an industry works and needs improvement, or if you want to use legal processes to reshape the world, then practicing administrative law may be for you. Virtually every aspect of public policy is addressed by one administrative agency or another. Topics include immigration, telecommunications, energy projects, environmental protection, food safety, securities and commodity trading, banking regulation, building codes, zoning, social security, utility rates, customs, and so on.

Basic questions to consider when facing an administrative law issue.

When a client approaches you to look at an issue that is or will be before an administrative agency, you need to consider issues somewhat differently from a two-party dispute which will be resolved by a court or arbitrator. The following check list attempts to highlight some of the broad questions you need to think about.

1. What is the problem as your client sees it?

    a. What is the regulatory action that has or may occur — a general rule, an action directed specifically at your client, what?

    b. Is your client comprehensively regulated by the agency (e.g., a utility) or is it concerned about regulations or actions affecting only a specific part of its business (*e.g.*, environmental or financial).

    c. How will it be affected directly and indirectly?

    d. Does your client have a view of how the perceived problem could or should be fixed?

    e. Does the agency misunderstand or exaggerate the problem it is trying to solve?

    f. Are there better ways the agency can achieve its goals?

2. What statutes, regulations, and policies are being implemented or considered by the agency and how would they apply?

    a. What broad and specific regulations, policies, and proposals are relevant to your client's situation?

    b. Do the agency's proposed actions fit within the statute and its existing regulations?

    c. Are your client's concerns valid?

    d. Can your client's concerns realistically be resolved within the existing or proposed legal and policy framework and, if not, what changes would be needed and what official or body could make those changes?

     e.   What facts would you need to show and what arguments would you need to make to bring about a favorable result for your client?

3.   Regulatory issues are not just about your client: who else is affected by the current regulations or the proposed action or your client's proposed solution?

     a.   Who else may benefit from or be hurt by the agency's regulations or proposed action or by your client's proposed solution?

     b.   Is your client's problem unique to its situation or is it a general problem for a sector of an industry? Might there be allies who could help persuade the agency?

     c.   How would the public at large be affected by your client's proposed solution to the agency proposal? Can the agency plausibly be persuaded that the changes would be beneficial to the public?

     d.   What are the politics surrounding the issue, if the matter rises to the level of political attention?

4.   What do you know about the agency that is asserting jurisdiction?

     a.   Under what statutory authority is it proposing to act and what discretion is afforded to the agency?

     b.   What kind of agency is it and how does it work? Is it independent or embedded in the executive branch?

     c.   How is it organized and how does it make its decisions (*e.g.*, single administrator or a commission that rules by majority)?

     d.   What are its rules of procedures and how would they apply to your client's situation?

     e.   Does it have enforcement or penalty authority that could come into play?

     f.   Are there other federal, state, or local agencies with authority over the same or related matters? Do their regulations or potential actions impose contradictory or complementary burdens on your client?

5.   What is the procedural context of your client's concern?

     a.   Does it face a complaint, an investigation, or an enforcement action with a possible penalty?

     b.   Is there an open proceeding in which the issues can or will be resolved? If so, what is its status and who initiated it?

     c.   Is your client seeking to change an existing rule or policy?

     d.   What procedural timeline has been established or is expected? In particular, is there a deadline either for your client's next move or for final agency action?

    e.   How can you present your facts and arguments to the agency? Do you need an expert witness?

    f.   Can you approach agency officials informally to clarify the proposal or the procedures or address the merits of issues?

6.   Would it be better for your client to fight or for it to try to bring its actions into compliance with the agency's current rules and policies?

    a.   What are the potential consequences of not changing its practices?

    b.   What are the prospects of winning a fight?

7.   Has your client already committed a violation of a law, regulation, or policy?

    a.   What legal, ethical, or moral duty does it have to inform the agency or the public?

    b.   Even if it has no duty, would there be a benefit of informing the agency? If so, how best to do it?

8.   How can you get access to the agency's rules and decisions?

    a.   Does it have a website?

    b.   Is there a reason to invoke the Freedom of Information Act (FOIA) or other public records laws to get more information about the agency's actions or policies?

9.   Are there potential allies who could help your client?

    a.   Are there legislators who may be interested in modifying the legal framework or in helping your client deal with the agency?

    b.   If other state or federal agencies have an interest in the same issues would those agencies' jurisdiction or policies be affected by the action that concerns your client? Could they be enlisted to help your client?

    c.   Would your client benefit by going to court? Is that premature? What steps would be needed to go to court? What issues could be raised? What court(s) would have jurisdiction?

These questions will occur and reoccur in a variety of administrative law settings. The problems that follow will attempt to expose you to several different contexts in which administrative law is developed or applied: adjudication, rulemaking, judicial review, information and some new, emerging public/private, hybrid contexts as well.

INTRODUCTION TO THE EXERCISES

The exercises presented in the succeeding chapters are intended to get you thinking about how to approach various administrative law issues which may be presented to you by your future clients. Necessarily, the problems below will be posed in particular administrative law contexts since the goal of the book is to help you get a feel for how administrative law principles and procedures are applied in practice.

For the sake of simplicity, we have tried to focus the exercises on a limited range of agencies and regulatory structures. As a result, some of the exercises will be built upon a limited range of factual and regulatory settings which will be spun out over the course of the book. An alternative would have been to emphasize a wider diversity of contexts, which might give you a better sense of the myriad areas in which regulatory policies and administrative law issues may affect your clients. However, we concluded that the investment you would have to make in learning substantive background for each of the problems would outweigh the benefit of such broad diversity.

Enough information is supplied in the text, the book's Appendix, and on the **LEXISNEXIS WEBCOURSE** to establish a problem and its context. Unless the problem calls for further research, you can rely on the information supplied by the book and on the webcourse, plus your readings in class, to answer the questions presented. However, please understand that the point of the exercises is to give you a *flavor* for practicing administrative law, not to make you a substantive expert in any particular area of federal or state regulation.

For the sake of manageability and simplicity, the examples will often involve a mix of real and hypothetical policies, decisions, and factual situations. The materials included should not be taken as definitive summary of the current state of any agency's policies, and hypothetical decisions should not be blamed on any real agency. In some problems, we have simplified the policy and its history and made up hypothetical decisions so you can focus on the administrative law issue, not the policy issues. Even where actual decisions are quoted (in whole or part), the decisions themselves may have been superseded before this book is published or revised.

In short, these are *exercises*. If you find a particular area of substantive regulation to be interesting, you may wish to pursue it in greater depth in another course or in your career.

Ask your professor whether the exercises should be done individually or whether you may work with others. In our view, the problems may be productively approached either way. Collaboration may enable you to cover more material and learn from exchanging ideas and drafts, but learning will be enhanced only if all of the collaborators take responsibility for sharing in the effort.

Note that the time estimates for problems are rough guides, which do not include time for reading the text or discussion with classmates. It is reasonable to expect that a polished product submitted for a grade will take longer than an outline prepared for a self-assessment.

PART ONE

ADMINISTRATIVE ADJUDICATION

OVERVIEW

We tend to take our models for administrative adjudication from state and federal courts. And these models do set forth many important fundamental issues regarding the process by which administrative orders are issued. As we shall see, however, the judicial model of adjudication is not the only model we have available. Administrative adjudication can and usually does differ in many ways. These differences involve the nature of the decision makers involved, the wide range of issues that are considered to be adjudicatory in nature, and, consequently, the flexibility and wide range of the adjudicatory procedures that may come into play. In some settings, such as in agency enforcement actions, administrative adjudication will look very much like the processes we are familiar with in state and federal court. In others, the processes will be more informal in nature but presumably enough to ensure fairness and a reasonably accurate decision. And in most instances, instead of a neutral, generalist judge that is used to adjudicating a wide range of substantive issues in federal or state court, agency adjudication is more specialized. The administrative decision makers involved may have seen scores if not hundreds of very similar cases. They are expected to be impartial, but they experts as well. Moreover, they will have not only technical expertise to bring to bear on the issues involved, but they will also be extremely familiar with the statutes involved as well as the agency's interpretation of those statutes.

The Administrative Procedure Act (a copy of which is available on line) divides its procedural world between adjudication and rulemaking or, more specifically, between rules and orders. We shall examine rulemaking in Part two. In this Part, we shall assume we are dealing with adjudications that ultimately will result in some kind of an administrative order.

Orders generally encompass decisions that are individual in nature, turn on facts that are retrospective in nature and are susceptible to evidentiary proof contained in a record upon which a decision is made. That decision will usually have findings of fact and conclusions of law, and it will give reasons for its ultimate outcome. When the formal adjudicative provisions of the APA are triggered, those proceedings can look very similar to what we are used to seeing in state and federal courts. Sections 554, 556 and 557 of the APA call for a hearing on the record, before an impartial judge, which allows for direct and cross examination and produces an order based on that record. Once a case is set for a formal hearing, the matter will proceed with many of the attributes of civil litigation. Other actions that do not trigger those APA provisions may constitute informal adjudication such as the proceedings considered in section 555(e) of the APA. Licensing, for example, will often require far less process than a formal hearing, but nonetheless require an agency decision based on reasons made contemporaneously with the decision. *Post hoc* rationalizations will not do. The expertise of the agency must be shown to have been involved when the actual decision was in fact made.

Moreover, many federal statutes simply require an agency to hold a "hearing" or sometimes a "public hearing" is mandated, but the magic words "on the record" are not used. This wording leaves in doubt whether the agency must use formal adjudicatory proceedings or can craft procedures that are less extensive. Increasingly, courts tend to defer to the agency's interpretation of its own statute even when procedures are involved. If the agency decides that the statute does not require formal proceedings, it is then free to set forth in its own regulations what the hearing or the public hearing will involve. These proceedings are often more than the informal processes used in a licensing or other kind of application proceeding, but less than the processes required by sections 554, 556 and 557.

Lurking in the background with all of these statutorily required adjudicatory proceedings are the constitutional due process requirements of the Fifth and Fourteenth amendments. (Portions of the U. S. Constitution are on line.) The Due Process Clause states that "no state shall deprive any person of life, liberty or property" without Due Process of law. For this provision to apply administratively there must be a property or a liberty interest at stake. In these adjudicatory contexts there always is, but the process required by the statute or the agency's own regulations usually satisfies due process concerns at the federal level. This is because the Due Process Clause establishes a floor and not a ceiling when it comes to how much process an agency must provide. Still, there invariably will be areas that were overlooked and that affect outcomes in serious ways. For example, if an adjudicatory proceeding turns on certain factual assumptions and one of the litigants sought some modified discovery to learn those facts, does the Due Process Clause require that discovery process be provided? Similarly, formal adjudicatory provisions under the APA have elaborate *ex parte* restrictions that must be followed. But are *ex parte* rules in play if formal adjudication is not triggered? What is the legal basis of any requirements that may be applied in the absence of a statute or the agency's own regulations?

The problems that follow are designed to illuminate some of the issues involved in agency adjudication. The problems begin with a basic illustration of how to find an agency's rules and regulations governing the issues that confront your client. Learning how to navigate individual agency web sites to understand how best to make your client's case is important for any lawyer practicing administrative law.

Practicing administrative law requires a lawyer to understand both policy and procedural contexts. A lawyer must develop strategies designed to navigate the established policies and procedures or to consider how one might change the policies in order to benefit one's client.

Rules and precedent are important but do not end the inquiry — administrative policies can evolve over time. An agency's rules are binding on it unless it takes steps to change the rules or it reasonably reinterprets them. Similarly, an agency must adhere to its precedents unless it concludes, based on a record of decision and a rational explanation of its actions, that a change of policy is justified and permitted by law.

A regulatory framework that made sense to a federal agency in one era of regulation may not make sense today. Changes may be due to new technology, new information on existing rules' shortcomings or changing views on how to balance economic, environmental or social values or other factors. Understanding the competing and evolving policies is critical to interpreting the words of a statute or regulation and to planning your strategy. Thus, if you can persuade a regulator that, in light of all the relevant factors, the public interest warrants *and* the law permits a change of course, then you have a shot at changing the policy to your client's — and, hopefully, the public's — advantage.

Importantly, each agency has its own procedural rules for seeking or opposing actions. Some are very formal with full discovery, motions, trial-type litigation, and briefing. But, often, issues are contested through less-formal processes, which may entail "paper hearings." Settlement processes may come into play as well. These may be initiated by the agency or by the parties themselves. Informal consultations with an agency's staff or decision makers may be permitted, but a practitioner must be very careful not to violate *ex parte* contact prohibitions. If unfavorable policies are embedded in existing regulations, you may need to seek to change the regulations themselves. That would entail a rulemaking.

In the end, being realistic with a client is vital. The odds of getting a desired result through an agency proceeding range from high to non-existent. It may be important to consider whether other options — legislative or commercial or other — might help the client achieve some, if not all, of its goals.

Chapter 1

GETTING STARTED: ADMINISTRATIVE ADJUDICATION

ESTIMATED TIME FOR COMPLETION: 60 minutes

ESTIMATED LEVEL OF DIFFICULTY: Easy

As your textbook and classes reveal, administrative law is built upon many layers of constitutional, statutory and judicial doctrines. However, in the day-to-day practice of administrative law, all problems begin with an individual client's problem(s), a statutory regime, and a particular agency's regulations and procedural rules.

This initial exercise starts from that basic proposition and introduces you to a common problem faced by practicing lawyers — how to get started on a problem involving a specific regulatory agency. A client (or a senior attorney) approaches the lawyer with a question in area of regulatory law that is new to the lawyer. It is up to the lawyer to understand the problem, gain a sense of the issues, and, then, find the agency's rules and policies in time to give the client a reasonable answer to its questions. The doctrinal issues will come along, but first you need to understand the agency.

The Client Calls . . .

Bob Marshall, the General Manager of the Town of Homersville's gas utility calls to make an appointment to discuss a problem Homersville faces and to see what it can do to address it.

Mr. Marshall explains that the Town of Homersville owns and operates a small municipal gas utility, which serves residents and businesses in the city. Homersville Gas is not regulated by either the Federal Energy Regulatory Commission ("FERC")[1]

---

[1] The Federal Energy Regulatory Commission, commonly known as "FERC," regulates facilities, rates and services of transporters of natural gas in interstate commerce, as well as some sellers of natural gas for resale (*i.e.*, at the wholesale level), under the Natural Gas Act (NGA), 15 U.S.C. Section 717. (Regulation of pipelines under the Natural Gas Policy Act (NGPA) is not relevant for purposes of the problems in this book.) Interstate pipeline regulation under the NGA is considered to be comprehensive regulation.

or by the State's Public Utility Commission.[2] "Homersville Gas" is a city department and its rates and services are established subject to approval by the city of Homersville's town council. It serves roughly 5,000 residential customers, plus municipally owned buildings, a hospital, schools, some small retail customers, apartment buildings, and one large manufacturer. The manufacturer uses as much natural gas as the rest of the customers combined.

You ask the nature of the issue and Mr. Marshall says that Homersville is in danger of losing its largest customer, Fantastic Manufacturing, which would cost the utility more than one million dollars each year. Mr. Marshall explains that Fantastic has announced a plan for North Central Gas Pipeline Company ("North Central") to build a 1.2-mile pipeline to connect directly to Fantastic's manufacturing plant. Fantastic's press release says the company can achieve substantial energy cost savings by "bypassing" Homersville's gas utility. Fantastic says that it has signed contracts for a pipeline interconnection with North Central and that, after the connection is made, it will purchase natural gas from an independent marketer of natural gas. Fantastic's press release asserts that North Central will commence construction of the 1.2-mile pipeline in the next six months and hopes to have service in place within nine months, shortly before its current, firm service contract with Homersville expires.

Loss of its largest customer, Mr. Marshall tells you, will force Homersville to significantly raise natural gas rates to its other customers or to raise its taxes. Everyone, including the school system and hospital, will see significant increases in their heating bills. He says it is bad enough that Homersville will lose approximately $500,000 in net revenues, which currently help reduce charges to other customers, but Homersville Gas will be stuck, for five more years, with a larger transportation contract with North Central than it will need. The cost to Homersville of the excess capacity will be approximately $600,000. It really "steams" him that the interstate pipeline "tricked" Homersville into signing the new long-term contract just before announcing that it was about to take away Homersville's biggest customer.

To make matters even worse, he says, the new pipeline will go through the town's nature park and bird sanctuary (the "Homersville Bird Sanctuary"), which is very popular with many local citizens. The sanctuary is roughly a mile across. It consists of roughly a quarter-mile ring of forest surrounding a meadow that is roughly one-half mile in diameter. The pipeline right of way will be 75 feet wide and remain permanently cleared of trees. Mr. Marshall has been told that interstate pipelines can exercise eminent domain to build any pipeline facilities certificated by the FERC. The land value, he says, cannot begin to capture the value of the parkland to the community and the wildlife that use it. There have been a number of recent sightings of an

---

Interstate transporters' rates and services must be "just and reasonable" and not "unduly discriminatory" and new facilities and service must be certificated based on FERC's finding that they are required by the "public convenience and necessity." In recent decades, case-by-case review of projects has been largely supplanted by a market-oriented, rule-based form of regulation, which allows regulated pipelines some freedom of competitive action within a set of regulatory boundaries. Nevertheless, pipelines' rates and some contested projects must be reviewed on a case-by-case basis. Publicly owned distributors of natural gas are not regulated by FERC.

[2] Some states regulate municipal utilities. Others do not. Nearly all states regulate investor-owned local utilities, which are generally known as local gas distribution companies.

endangered bird species in the Homersville Bird Sanctuary, he says.

This is not your practice area, but you recall that interstate natural gas pipelines are regulated by FERC under the Natural Gas Act ("NGA"). Interstate natural gas pipelines are federally regulated because they build and operate pipelines that cross state lines and they often have monopoly power over their customers and potential customers. They have economic power both because of their size and configuration and because regulation potentially limits the number of new entrants. Interstate gas pipelines often extend hundreds or even thousands of miles between production areas (*e.g.*, in the Southwestern U.S. or Canada) and markets (*e.g.*, in the Midwest and Atlantic States). Pipeline customers, like Homersville, may be connected to a single pipeline and have few supply alternatives. Thus, in the 1930s, Congress enacted comprehensive regulation of interstate pipelines whose activities were infused with the public interest.

You also recall generally that, under the NGA, FERC regulates the construction and operation of interstate pipelines through a process of issuing "certificates of public convenience and necessity" if it determines that the proposed construction and services will serve the public interest. All factors relevant to the public interest may be considered by FERC. Interstate pipelines' contracts, rates and tariffs must be shown to be "just and reasonable" and not "unduly discriminatory." Lastly, you recall reading that FERC's mode of regulation in recent years has been to promote the public interest by encouraging competition among gas sellers and transporters within a framework designed to prevent abuses of pipelines' market power. To that end, FERC's modern policies require interstate pipelines to transport natural gas owned by shippers on an "open access" basis.

After Mr. Marshall gives you a general description of the problem, you ask Mr. Marshall a few questions which come to mind immediately and then arrange a meeting.

EXERCISE 1A — INITIAL QUESTIONS TO YOUR CLIENT

What questions for Mr. Marshall immediately come to mind while you are still on the phone? Make a list of your initial questions.

The key at this initial stage is for you, as the lawyer, to try to get enough information about the client's situation, concerns, and objectives so you can prepare adequately for the meeting to come and avoid overlooking key issues that might arise. Obviously, you will be able to ask more questions and independently investigate the facts as the case develops, but the initial meeting is important to creating a strategy and to managing your client's expectations about what may be plausible. Even 5 or 10 minutes of initial Q&A with your client during your first conversation can save you a lot of time narrowing the issues and developing an appropriate strategy. It will make your first face-to-face meeting that much more effective.

In posing your initial questions, your thinking would be much as in other dispute contexts: you want to be sure you understand who the players are; how they relate to each other; what your client's concerns are; who else may be helped or hurt by the agency's granting or denying the contemplated project (or rate increase or license or permit or whatever); and what your client wants to achieve. In other words, much as in other dispute contexts, you want to figure out as quickly as possible whose interests will be helped, whose will be hurt, and how?

Since this issue involves administrative law, you also want to think about the public impacts and policy considerations that might be raised by your client's predicament. In addition to the equities between the immediate parties, how will the public be helped or hurt? What public policies may be affected or applicable? Even before you know the specific statutory and regulatory framework, you will likely have an intuitive sense of the policy issues that may arise.

EXERCISE 1B — FINDING THE APPLICABLE AGENCY RULES AND ORDERS

The next step is to learn about the agency. Not all agencies are structured the same way. This exercise will help you dig into one agency's structure, rules, and practices. Note that this exercise is intentionally limited in scope. In practice, you would need to do much more substantive and procedural research before meeting with your client. The goal here is to focus on the procedural side of the equation and to introduce readily available tools to answering the start-up questions.

To make it easier for you to understand the substantive legal context, we will provide substantive background as the exercises move forward. For now, you need simply to be aware that "your recollection" as summarized above is correct. North Central is regulated, under the Natural Gas Act, as a "natural gas company" because it transports natural gas in interstate commerce. As such, its rates, contracts, services, and facilities are regulated by the Federal Energy Regulatory Commission. Its rates, contracts, and services must be just and reasonable and not unduly discriminatory. It must get prior approval of a "certificate of public convenience and necessity" in order to construct pipeline facilities, including the type of facility contemplated by North Central to serve Fantastic. FERC has adopted blanket certificate regulations that permit pipelines to construct low-cost facilities, subject to standard conditions, provided that no one protests the proposed construction.

a. Using Lexis-Nexis or the General Printing Office's electronic version of the Code of Federal Regulations ("e-CFR" is at http://ecfr.gpoaccess.gov/), locate FERC's rules of practice and procedure governing motions to intervene and protests. In this regard, FERC's rules of practice and procedure can be found at 18 C.F.R. Part 385. The rules governing interventions and protests at FERC are in Part 385, Subpart B, Rules 211–217, and the rules concerning formats for filings are in Subpart T. Rules governing construction projects of the sort proposed by North Central can be found at 18 C.F.R. Part 157, Subpart F, with Sections 157.205, .206, .211(a)(2) being particularly relevant to the exercises in this book. The gist of those rules is that a pipeline holding a blanket certificate can construct delivery points and related facilities (157.211), subject to prior notice and protest procedures (157.205) and to compliance with standard environmental conditions (157.206).

b. Review the rules that are of particular importance to filing a motion to intervene and protest.

c. Go on FERC's website (www.ferc.gov) and look at how the agency is organized. Then, find the record of a pipeline proceeding in which interventions and protests have been filed. This is a useful exercise because one quick way to gain entry into an administrative practice area in which you are unfamiliar is to look at the record of other cases. There, you can see how the agency and more experienced practitioners have addressed issues. You can also find examples of pleadings which may be useful as models for form even if not for substance.

As an illustration, go to FERC's website — www.ferc.gov. Next, go to

"Documents and Filings"; then to "ELibrary"; then to "General Search." In "General Search," pick a date range from 2006 to present and type CP07-79 into the space for the docket number. Hit Submit.

Look over the issuances by the agency and the types of pleadings that have been filed by both sides. The submissions should give you an idea how pleadings are prepared and submitted to an administrative agency. Of course, other agencies will have their own rules of procedure and the precise formats may vary, but these filings should still give you an idea of how a contested adjudication will play out, in the absence of a formal hearing.

d.   Find one other certificate docket in which interventions and protests have been filed. To do this, initiate a similar search, except rather than the full docket number, simply type "CP10" or "CP09" in the docket entry; in the box for "Text Search," type "protest"; and then check the adjacent small box for "Description."

Chapter 2

PREPARING A MOTION TO INTERVENE AND PROTEST

ESTIMATED TIME FOR COMPLETION: 90 minutes

ESTIMATED LEVEL OF DIFFICULTY: Moderate

Adjudicative proceedings can begin in several ways. Frequently, they are initiated by the filing of an application for a permit or rate change by a regulated entity. They might also be initiated by the filing of a complaint or an order to show cause. In the exercise below, your client is able to intervene in the FERC proceeding, protest the filing, and request rejection or hearings. Your job will be to work with your client to develop and implement a strategy.

When you meet with Mr. Marshall, you explain to him the results of your research, including your review of North Central's application (see Appendix for use with Chapters 1–5), and you seek to further explore the issues and your client's objectives.

You have confirmed that the case arises under Section 7(c) of the Natural Gas Act (15 U.S.C. 717f(c)), which is under the jurisdiction of the Federal Energy Regulatory Commission. The NGA places the burden of proof on the pipeline to demonstrate that its proposed project is "required by the public convenience and necessity." The NGA empowers FERC to place conditions on certificates in order to assure that the public interest is not harmed. Once a certificate authorizing construction is issued, Section 7(h) authorizes the pipeline to invoke the power of eminent domain in order to take land in exchange for compensation determined appropriate by a court.

Over the years, judicial decisions have required FERC to consider *nearly all factors* that might affect the public interest when it evaluates an application for a certificate of public convenience and necessity. Among the many factors it must consider are potential impacts on customers, economic-development benefits, improved access to natural gas, environmental impacts, antitrust policies, customers' desires, harm to third parties including competitors, pipeline safety, consistency with FERC's established policies, etc. FERC may impose certificate conditions to mitigate

21

the harms that might otherwise result from a proposal (*e.g.*, ordering a change of route, restricting construction techniques or timing to mitigate environmental impacts, modifying a project's size, limiting or expanding the services to be provided, allowing an existing customer to turn back capacity it no longer needs, etc.).

You explain that you have reached several preliminary conclusions from your research.

(1) In order to reduce regulatory burdens, FERC has issued "blanket certificates" to interstate pipelines, including North Central, authorizing a variety of kinds of common construction projects, subject to standard conditions and dollar limitations. *Unless* a *protest is filed*, the blanket certificate rules will automatically approve North Central's proposal to build the new pipeline and delivery point to serve Fantastic and "bypass" services rendered by Homersville. After North Central's application was filed, FERC published a notice of the application in the Federal Register, giving the public 60 days to intervene and protest the application. If a protest is filed, FERC will review the application and protest(s) (assuming the parties do not reach a settlement within 30 days) and either make a decision on the merits or set the matter for further procedures. [Relevant portions of these regulations are included on the **LEXISNEXIS WEBCOURSE**.]

(2) FERC has a "pro-competition" policy which allows customers, such as Fantastic, to choose their suppliers and requires pipelines, like North Central, to transport natural gas for current and potential customers on a non-discriminatory basis to the extent there is available transportation capacity. Over the past 20 years, FERC's decisions in individual cases consistently approve "bypasses" over the economic objections of local distributors. FERC's policy is that the public interest will be best served by competition and that customers' choices should be honored. The courts have consistently affirmed FERC's decisions approving bypass projects proposed by interstate pipelines. Consequently, North Central's proposal is unlikely to be blocked solely based on the possible economic harm to Homersville. [The decision you encountered in FERC Docket No. CP07-79-000, in Exercise 1B(c), spells out FERC's policy on bypass.]

(3) NGA Sections 4 and 5 (15 U.S.C. §§ 717c, 717d) require pipelines rates and contracts to be "just and reasonable" and not unduly discriminatory. FERC has held that it will act to prevent unreasonable or discriminatory treatment of customers or "unfair competition" or unfair exercises of a pipeline's monopoly power, as well as any direct violations of its blanket certificate rules. Here, FERC might be receptive to an argument that North Central deceived Homersville into an expensive, extension of its transportation contract just before announcing that it was going to take Homersville's largest customer. Such behavior might be viewed as "unjust and unreasonable."

(4) The potential harm to the bird sanctuary, public users of the sanctuary and any endangered or threatened species in a protest are all relevant to a determination of whether the proposal will serve the public convenience and necessity. Such environmental harms could cause FERC to reject North

Central's proposal as being contrary to the public interest, or they might cause FERC to condition its approval upon the applicant's developing a new route that avoids the bird sanctuary. The National Environmental Policy Act of 1969 (42 U.S.C. § 4321 *et seq.*) ("NEPA") (available on the **LEXISNEXIS WEBCOURSE**) requires a federal agency, such as FERC, to prepare an environmental impact statement for proposed actions that would significantly affect the environment. NGA Section 15 (15 U.S.C. § 717n) makes FERC the "lead agency" for NEPA reviews of pipeline projects. In addition, FERC is required to consult with the U.S. Fish and Wildlife Service concerning any potential adverse impacts on endangered species or their habitats. FERC has delegated the consultation process to blanket certificate holders, such as North Central, deeming them to be its "non-Federal representative" to the USFWS. (18 C.F.R. Part 157, Subpart F, App. I.) According to Appendix 2 of its application, North Central apparently relied on a 2009 letter from USFWS without any updated consultation or investigation of potential endangered species in the area.

(5) As Mr. Marshall feared, a certificate of public convenience and necessity carries with it the power of eminent domain (enforced through the courts), pursuant to Section 7(h) of the Natural Gas Act. Consequently, if FERC approves construction through the bird sanctuary, a district court considering a suit to exercise eminent domain will not review FERC's decision but will only enforce it and award appropriate compensation.

You also tell Mr. Marshall that FERC's notice of the application (see Appendix) appeared in the Federal Register two weeks ago and that interventions and protests are due to be filed in six weeks.

You confirm with Mr. Marshall all the facts he told you previously (in Chapter 1).

Mr. Marshall emphasizes that the bird sanctuary would be severely harmed by a construction project that clears a 75-foot right of way through the middle of the meadow and through a quarter mile of forest on each side of the meadow. The sanctuary, which is roughly 500 acres, is regularly used as a nature park by the town's citizens, and it attracts tourists to the area. Even if the boardwalk and trails can be restored and new meadows planted, the visual impacts and habitat damage from permanent removal of trees are irreparable. Local birdwatchers claim to have seen an endangered species of bird (William's Flycatcher) on multiple occasions in the last two years. He understands that the bird depends on forested areas.

Mr. Marshall notes that North Central could build a 5-mile pipeline outside the sanctuary, next to a railroad, in order to reach Fantastic Manufacturing. That would avoid going through the sanctuary, but it would likely cost more to build than Fantastic wants to pay for the bypass.

You identify the possible rulings FERC might make and ask about the outcomes he would like to see. You explain that, substantively, (a) FERC could reject the application as contrary to the public convenience and necessity or possibly because the application failed to demonstrate meaningful consultation with the USFWS; (b) FERC could approve the project as proposed; or (c) FERC could approve the project subject to conditions (*e.g.*, requiring the route to avoid the bird sanctuary or allowing Homersville to turnback the uneeded portion of its new contract with North Central). Procedurally, it could act based on the pleadings (its usual preference), set the matter for a "technical conference,"[1] or order an evidentiary hearing before an administrative law judge.

Mr. Marshall asks you to file papers with FERC objecting to the project. He wants to fight the project and get a hearing before FERC. He asserts that his first choice would be to block the project altogether. That would protect the bird sanctuary and his customer base. As fallback positions, he would like the pipeline to re-route its construction outside the sanctuary and he would like to reduce the size of his new contract with North Central by the amount of the load he is going to lose.

After conferring with Mr. Marshall, you contact a biology professor, Dr. Robin Nester, PhD, at the local state college to confirm that there have been sightings of an endangered species, in the last year or so, in the bird sanctuary. She says she has seen the bird (William's Flycatcher) on several occasions and she has been told that local birders have seen it on other occasions. She saw a male and a female together on one occasion in the Spring and two males on other occasions. Spring is the time for nesting, so nesting is possible; however, she has not seen a nest. This species favors forests but occasionally flies into meadows for insects. In her opinion, disturbance of the sanctuary would adversely affect this endangered species and disrupt nesting if it is going on. She is working on a paper but has not yet submitted it for publication. Although the sightings are well known among local birders, she is concerned that extensive publicity could attract people who might harm the birds. She has alerted the superintendant of the bird sanctuary and an official at the U.S. Fish and Wildlife Service of the sightings. She did not know the name of the USFWS official and she did not mention the possible construction because she did not know of it at the time.

Dr. Nester adds that she is the president of the Homersville Audubon Society, which has 80 members, all of whom regularly utilize the sanctuary. The group leads trips for its members and the general public. Harm to the sanctuary would be a terrible loss for the community. Her affidavit concerning these issues is attached to the HAS Motion to Intervene and Protest in the Appendix.

---

[1] A "technical conference" is a procedural innovation by FERC. It consists of an informal meeting in which all parties can ask present their evidence and views to members of the Commission's advisory staff and ask each other questions. However, the conference does not result in a transcript or other reviewable record. Instead, parties are invited to file their presentations and any additional arguments or materials as part of the proceeding's written record, following the technical conference. The meeting will form part of the basis for the agency staff's recommendations to the Commissioners. Those recommendations may be in the form of a report that is open to the public or may be made in internal communications which are not published.

EXERCISE 2A — PREPARE A MOTION TO INTERVENE, PROTEST, AND REQUEST FOR HEARING

When you prepare a filing, such as a motion to intervene, protest, and request for hearing, you need to follow the applicable procedural rules; be sure that your factual assertions are accurate; clearly state the relief you are seeking; and array your facts and arguments as persuasively as possible. Note that FERC's rules indicate that attorneys, as well as certain other individuals, can file pleadings (Rule 2101) and that a signature on a pleading affirms the representative's authority to file, that the pleading has been read and its contents are known by the signer, and that "the contents are true as stated, to the best knowledge and belief of the signer" (Rule 2005).

For purposes of drafting the filing, review the facts set forth above and in the Appendix. Look at FERC's rules in the **LEXISNEXIS WEBCOURSE** (particularly 18 C.F.R. Part 385, Rules 203, 210–214, and Rules 2001–2010) and at one or more examples of motions to intervene and protests filed by parties in other cases. For purposes of this exercise, you may look at previously filed pleadings as "go-by" models for basic form. While a full protest might be lengthy and might warrant attachment of an affidavit or other evidence, your draft may be more summary in character, perhaps 5-10 pages double space.

As you are drafting keep the following questions in mind:

(a) What standing does Homersville have to intervene in a FERC certificate proceeding?

(b) What are the elements you must include in the filing?

(c) What arguments would you make for rejecting the application or for a hearing or other procedures?

(d) What relief would you request?

(e) Who must you serve with the filing?

(f) What additional facts would you like to know in order to strengthen your pleading?

EXERCISE 2B — OTHER POTENTIAL INTERVENORS

Four other potential parties approach you to express their interest in intervening and protesting. Like Homersville, they oppose North Central's proposed project. The entities are:

1. **The Homersville Audubon Society.** Its members routinely use the Homersville Bird Sanctuary. Since the sanctuary was founded in 1960, the Society and its members have provided maintenance support (removal of trash and noxious species of plants from the refuge), led bird-watching trips, and offered educational outings to its members and the public. All they have done has been out of their love for the sanctuary, not for profit. Construction of a pipeline and clearing of a right-of-way through the heart of the refuge would harm its members' and the public's enjoyment of the sanctuary and could drive off an endangered species of bird, William's Flycatcher.

2. **The Homersville Taxpayers Alliance.** The Taxpayers Alliance generally advocates minimization of taxes and efficient public use of tax revenues. Its members pay taxes to the Town of Homersville for a variety of purposes, including maintenance of the bird sanctuary. The group's president, Mr. Hugo Leep, tells you that the group is disturbed that a private entity (the pipeline) can exercise eminent domain (NGA Section 7(h)) to take a portion of the sanctuary in order to serve a single private company which already gets natural gas from Homersville. The Alliance's members have been paying good tax dollars for 20 years, he says, and they will be deprived of the sanctuary for which they have been paying those taxes. "I don't care about the birds and bees there," he adds, "but I do care about a waste of our tax dollars." The city and its citizens will get virtually nothing in the way of a payment for the easement. Compensation, he says, will probably be based on uncultivated, rural land when it is worth a lot more than that to the community." He says a few of the group's members visit the sanctuary, and some buy natural gas from Homersville and might also see rate increases.

3. **The International Birders Union.** The IBU is an international association of bird watchers including a number of U.S. residents. IBU's members visit parks, refuges, and other locations in the U.S. and around the world in search of rare birds. The IBU's statement of organizational purpose strongly supports the formation and preservation of bird sanctuaries. No member is known to have visited the Homersville Bird Sanctuary, but some members have visited other sanctuaries in search of the remaining examples of William's Flycatcher, which is a migratory species.

4. **Mid-Central Pipeline Company**. Mid-Central has an interstate pipeline that runs ten miles from the Fantastic Manufacturing plant. It does not currently serve either Fantastic or Homersville, but it asserts that it could build a line to either Fantastic or Homersville along a route that would avoid going through the bird sanctuary. Although its construction costs would be much higher than North Central's proposed route through the sanctuary, its alternative would benefit the environment by avoiding the sanctuary.

Two issues are raised by these entities.

First, would each have standing to intervene *at the agency level*?

Second, could you represent more than one party to the proceeding without encountering conflicts concerning positions that the parties wish to take? Your thinking about the second issue raises questions about the likelihood of there being future conflicting positions (either in litigation or settlement), and whether you can reach agreements at the outset about how to avoid or resolve potential conflicts (*e.g.*, in positions, strategies, or settlement) if they were to arise.

Without undertaking an exhaustive review at this time, how would you answer or go about answering the two questions? Think about these questions and jot down the practical advice you would you give Homersville about (1) the chances that the three entities could successfully intervene in the case and (2) the advisability of Homersville's consenting to joint representation?

Chapter 3

WHAT PROCESS IS DUE?

ESTIMATED TIME FOR COMPLETION: 90 minutes

ESTIMATED LEVEL OF DIFFICULTY: Difficult

A recurring question before an administrative agency, such as FERC, is to decide what procedures need to be followed in order to produce a fair and reasoned decision in compliance with the applicable statutes and judicial interpretations of those statutes. In federal cases, the Administrative Procedure Act establishes the foundation for much analysis. However, individual substantive statutes may set forth their own standards for procedural actions, and agencies may develop their own procedural requirements, which may go beyond the statutory minimums. As you can see in the Appendix and the **LEXISNEXIS WEBCOURSE**, the Natural Gas Act, for example, Section 19 (15 U.S.C. § 717r) requires that decisions be supported by "substantial evidence" and Section 15 (15 U.S.C. § 717n) permits the use of informal hearing procedures, provided that "appropriate records thereof shall be kept." FERC's stated policies call for evidentiary hearings as needed to resolve material issues of fact in adjudications. If a matter is set for an evidentiary hearing, the proceeding will follow processes before an administrative law judge, which would seem generally familiar to trial litigators, albeit with pre-filed, written testimony[1] and somewhat relaxed rules of evidence. In some cases, FERC will order settlement procedures, possibly mediated by a staff member or a "settlement judge" (an ALJ who will not be assigned to decide the case). If a settlement cannot be reached, the case will be decided on the pleadings or after an evidentiary hearing. FERC has also innovated with a technical conference process, which is more fully described below.

---

[1] Administrative agencies frequently use "pre-filed" written testimony, which is subject to discovery and cross-examination. The testimony is structured with questions, answers and, as appropriate, exhibits. The written testimony is accompanied by an affidavit. At the hearing before the ALJ, the testimony is introduced as evidence and accepted subject to cross-examination and possible motions to strike particular parts. Pre-filed testimony is deemed to be more efficient and sometimes more clear than live testimony. Issues of credibility and weaknesses in the testimony can be brought out through cross-examination.

EXERCISE 3A — MEMO RECOMMENDING APPROPRIATE PROCEDURES

You are the attorney-advisor to the Chair of the FERC. She has seen the interventions and protests, as well as North Central's motion for leave to reply. She asks for your advice on how to handle the application: what procedures do you recommend that the Commission follow in order to resolve the issues that have been raised by the application and other filings? She is not fond of delay or unnecessary use of agency resources, but she "wants to do the right thing" and does not want to be reversed.

You review the pipeline's filing and protests — which are included or summarized in the Appendix or you wrote in Exercise 2A — and find the following.

There are five protesting parties — Homersville, the Homersville Audubon Society, the International Birders Union, the Homersville Taxpayers Alliance, and Mid-Central Pipeline Company. Each has raised clear objections to the filing and has requested a formal evidentiary proceeding. The Homersville Audubon Society submitted Dr. Nester's affidavit with its protest. The first three argue that (a) the applicant failed to prove that the public interest will be served given the harm to the bird sanctuary, to the citizens who make extensive use of it, and to the endangered species which has been sighted there, and given the economic harm to Homersville and its other customers from the bypass; (b) North Central acted unfairly and unreasonably (and contrary to the public interest) by inducing Homersville to sign a contract extension without disclosing that it was taking Homersville's largest customer; (c) FERC must prepare an environmental impact statement ("EIS") that considers the environmental impacts and potential alternatives to the project; and (d) neither FERC nor North Central has properly assessed harm to the endangered species or consulted with the U.S. Fish and Wildlife Service concerning the damage. The protestors request a hearing and, ultimately, rejection or, alternatively, approval subject to conditions that re-route the pipeline outside the bird sanctuary and relieve Homersville of all or a portion of the extended contract. Mid-Central contends that it could provide service to Fantastic without going through the bird sanctuary.

You also review the filings by North Central and by Fantastic, which moved to intervene in support of North Central's application. They argue that the Commission should reject the protests and summarily approve the project. They assert that (a) FERC policies clearly permit bypasses, notwithstanding the alleged economic impact to traditional suppliers; (b) North Central should not have to modify the contract extension with Homersville, since it had no duty to alert Homersville to the prospective service to Fantastic and Homersville was not forced to extend its contract; (c) it would be too costly to re-route the pipeline around the bird sanctuary (mainly because of added distance and the expected low valuation for parkland); (d) it is a small, routine pipeline project which will adhere to FERC's standard requirements and is not worthy of an EIS; and (e) Homersville had not proven either that an endangered species was regularly present or that mitigating steps (timing of construction and construction techniques) would be inadequate or that cutting trees for the right-of-way would actually be harmful (since it could be attractive to deer and some other wildlife). They also object to Mid-Central's proposal as being too late and more costly than North Central's proposed bypass.

In broad terms, you agree with North Central that FERC's longstanding policies would permit "bypass" construction even to take a large customer away from a local distributor, such as Homersville. You cannot find a clear policy on a pipeline's extending a contract with a customer just before bypassing it, but it is not disputed that North Central negotiated the contract extension without disclosing that North Central was about to take Homersville's largest customer. As to the environmental impact, you find it hard to tell what the risks are from the pleadings. The agency staff's internal memorandum indicates that the staff was not aware that an endangered bird might be in the location but partial mitigation might be achieved by scheduling construction in winter months. No trees will be allowed ever to grow on the right of way. The cost of re-routing the pipeline is not clear, but any re-routing costs would be higher than the proposal and would be borne by Fantastic, unless the higher cost would kill the project. You are not sure how to balance costs to the pipeline against the risks to the park, the citizens, and the birdlife.

With those thoughts in mind, you can see four procedural options that the agency might pursue:

(1) Formal hearing. A full evidentiary hearing before an Administrative Law Judge (ALJ) would trigger the opportunity for discovery, the filing of prepared written testimony (direct, reply, and rebuttal), live cross-examination of witnesses, briefing to the ALJ, an "initial decision" by the ALJ, briefs on and opposing exceptions to the ALJ's decision, and a final Commission decision. This process would closely resemble civil litigation before a judge, except perhaps for some relaxation of evidentiary rules. A complete record would be compiled. It is the most expensive agency procedure for resolving issues for both the agency and the parties. The agency's litigation staff would participate and could assure that the record is complete.

(2) Technical Conference. FERC frequently conducts "technical conferences" to get more information in a case, instead of conducting full hearings. As conceived by FERC, a technical conference entails an informal, *off-the-record* meeting in which the parties can make presentations to the FERC *advisory staff* concerning the parties' positions on issues of fact and policy and on their recommended remedies. In addition to making their own presentations, parties are expected to answer questions from the agency staff, possibly with follow-up factual submissions if the staff requests them. Parties may ask questions of one another, but responses may or may not be complete. The staff listens to what is said and may make notes. Presentations are typically made by lawyers or company officials and are not under oath, although it is expected that parties will tell the truth. Following a technical conference, parties are invited to file written comments on the merits of the case. These comments may include the parties' presentations at the technical conference (with or

without amendments) and may comment further on the staff's questions or other parties' remarks. If they believe that more formal procedures are needed to resolve material factual issues, any party can request further procedures, such as a formal evidentiary hearing. However, FERC rarely sets a matter for hearing after conducting a technical conference. Following the conference and further presentations, the advisory staff either issues a formal report or makes confidential recommendations to the Commissioners concerning the appropriate outcome to the proceeding. The record consists entirely of the parties' written filings submitted before and after the technical conference and any orders or other documents issued by FERC or its staff.

(3) Summary agency action based on the pleadings. FERC's position is that it can act based on the pleadings if there are no disputed issues of material facts which require further procedures to resolve. Material facts are facts needed to make a decision in light of applicable statutory standards and the agency's current policies. If, for example, FERC's policies support approving a pipeline delivery project whenever the customer wants an interconnection and is willing to pay the cost of construction, then it would not be "material," in FERC's view, that the current supplier would lose a customer or suffer economic harm. On the other hand, disputes over other issues (e.g., environmental impacts) may require a decision on disputed issues of fact, in order to decide the broader public interest issue. In such cases, the agency may need to go beyond the filed pleadings in order to resolve the factual issues. Because the agency has considerable expertise concerning the operations of the regulated industry, it may be able to resolve some disputes by relying on that expertise.

(4) Initiating a settlement process before an ALJ or other agency employee. FERC, like many other agencies, likes to resolve issues by settlement where possible. If successful, a settlement process may resolve a proceeding with fewer resources and the agency can avoid having to decide the merits of a dispute. From the parties' vantage point, a tolerable compromise may be better than risking an intolerable ruling on the merits. Apart from simply inviting settlement negotiations, FERC has various mediation procedures available to help parties bring about a resolution. If the parties' positions offer no hope of a middle ground, a settlement process may be a waste of time.

Each of these procedures entails different claims upon the agency's and parties' resources and different risks of reversal upon appeal. Your boss does not like to commit agency resources unnecessarily.

In preparing your memorandum, consider the positions of the parties in this matter and the possible procedures outlined above. Are there disputed issues of material fact which cannot be resolved based upon the pleadings alone? Are there issues that can easily be resolved based on established policies? Is a technical conference an adequate procedure for resolving disputed facts, such as those relating to the endangered species? Would it be appropriate to use a combination of procedures (e.g., to resolve some issues on the pleadings and others through a hearing or technical conference or a combination of hearing and technical conference) or are the public interest issues intertwined so it would it be more appropriate to get a comprehensive recommended decision from an ALJ or the staff. Are the parties so far apart that a middle ground is unlikely to be found in a settlement process?

Setting aside the settlement option for the time being, outline a memo to the FERC Chair, briefly describing the pros and cons of each of the first three procedural options described above, including (a) the adequacy of each procedure to provide an accurate record for resolving the merits including the material issues raised by the parties, (b) the likelihood of withstanding judicial review, and (c) your own recommendation for which procedure you believe the agency should employ. Remember that, if the agency gets the choice of procedure wrong, someone may be unfairly harmed and, if the losing party seeks judicial review, the agency's decisional process will need to be defended.

Chapter 4

ADMINISTRATIVE SETTLEMENT PROCESSES

ESTIMATED TIME FOR COMPLETION: 60 minutes

ESTIMATED LEVEL OF DIFFICULTY: Moderate

Administrative agencies are generally big fans of settlement agreements, particularly in the adjudicative context. Settlements have become essential tools to resolve a wide range of adjudicative proceedings. For example, settlements resolve all or parts of many, if not most, rate proceedings before state and federal agencies that regulate utilities or pipelines. Settlements are also widely used to resolve enforcement proceedings in which an agency accuses a regulated company of violating applicable regulations.

Settlements before administrative agencies can arise in at least three contexts.

(1) Settlements are frequently negotiated in contested rate, tariff, licensing, or complaint proceedings. They are presented to an agency as a written agreement by the parties to resolve all or part of the issues in the proceeding. While no party may get everything it claimed it wanted, each consenting party gets a compromise it can live with. For example, a utility may get lower rates than it requested, but higher rates than the protesting parties originally recommended. Each party resolves its litigation risks within bounds acceptable to the agency.

(2) Sometimes, settlements are worked out in rulemaking contexts, in which generally applicable regulations are developed through discussion and compromise by different interest groups. This is the practical effect where the rulemaking adopts standards promulgated by an industry standard-setting organization in which the participants are drawn from companies interested in setting common protocols for communications, electronic transactions, standard contracts, or product specifications.

(3) Settlements are frequently reached in enforcement proceedings in which the agency accuses a regulated entity or individual of violating agency orders

or regulations or the underlying statute. Here, the agency and the respondent may work out a resolution which involves corrective actions or penalties or both. Ordinarily, like a plea agreement in a criminal proceeding, the settlement would set penalties below the maximum statutory level or perhaps waive them entirely. Settlement of an enforcement proceeding may also enable the respondent to resolve a complaint or investigation without admitting guilt and without the agency making a formal finding that would have collateral consequences in civil litigation or other agency proceedings.[*]

Since approval of the settlement will resolve some or all the issues in the proceeding, the agency will need to review the settlement and issue an order accepting or rejecting the compromise. To the extent the settlement sets rates or approves a project, the agency will likely still have to find that the settlement satisfies the statutory standards for new rates (*e.g.*, they are "just and reasonable") or new projects (*e.g.*, serves the "public interest"). For that, it may need a record with evidence supporting the settlement. If the agency is troubled by aspects of the settlement and cannot make the necessary statutory findings, the agency might also approve the settlement proposal subject to conditions which would modify or supplement the settlement's terms. Obviously, the parties to the settlement will need to write the settlement in a manner that protects themselves from agency modifications which would take away the bargain they have negotiated. Typically this is done by incorporating provisions which declare that the settlement will be deemed void and privileged if it is modified by the agency and the modifications are not accepted by all of the parties to the settlement.

Settlements have several obvious potential advantages.

Settlement processes allow parties to work out their own solutions to disputes, and thereby mitigate the risks of going to a litigated decision the outcome of which may be difficult to predict.

Settlements can reduce the agency's work load by reducing the need to devote staff resources to litigation and appeals.

Since settlements are generally viewed as non-precedential compromises, an agency may have freedom to accept resolutions which it would not be able to order consistently with its precedents. It can hold its nose so long as no one else is hurt and no statutory prohibition is violated.

On the other hand, settlements can also be a source of mischief.

Adverse public impacts. Statutes impose regulation on industries or individuals because private actions can have adverse public consequences. Unlike most purely private litigation, settlements between parties to a regulatory proceeding may adversely affect members of the public who are not parties to the proceeding. Those unrepresented parties — and the legislature — rely on the agency to look out for the public's interest. The danger of an imbalanced settlement can be significant since the

---

[*] On the LEXISNEXIS WEBCOURSE materials, you can find FERC's Rules of Practice and Procedure governing settlements, the Negotiated Rulemaking Act, and examples of settlements in agency enforcement and litigation contexts.

mix of participants in a case is often skewed toward large players which may come from a limited subset of the overall public.

One obvious example of the potential problems would be a rate-case settlement in which a utility and its big customers agree to let the utility achieve its revenue goals by raising rates to small, unrepresented customers, while keeping rates low for the active, big customers. The utility would raise as much money as it wants, and the settling parties would shift the costs largely to entities not participating in the case. All the *participants* would win, but the *public* would not. This is part of the reason that many States have full-time "consumer advocate" offices to represent small customers (typically residential and small commercial customers) who do not have the where-withal to participate in complex rate proceedings.

Another example of settlement requiring close scrutiny would be a licensing case in which competitors agree to conditions which would have the effect of impermissibly dividing the market and limiting competition or which would limit expected environmental protections. Just because the parties to the case reach an agreement does not mean that the public interest will be served by their resolution.

Compliance with statutory standards. Unless the agency has authority to waive the applicable statutory standards, the agency will still have to determine that a settlement satisfies applicable statutory standards. And, even if the agency could waive those statutory standards, it would need to explain why a waiver is acceptable and why an exception would not undermine the larger statutory scheme.

Apart from the terms of the statute, a proposed settlement may call for results inconsistent with the agency's published regulations and policies. While it may have some authority to waive its own regulations and announced policies, it cannot do so without giving serious consideration to the consequences. An agency needs to be careful not to allow settlements to circumvent regulatory policies, thereby weakening those policies and opening the doors to demands by others to be exempted.

Constraints on agency authority. In some circumstances, the agency itself may be deemed to be a party to the settlement in a way that might limit its ability to react to changing circumstances in the future. It is one thing to resolve a past violation through a settlement; it is another matter to limit an agency's future ability to address new problems. Consequently, an agency needs to assure that settlements do not restrict the agency's ability to protect the public interest in the future.

Agency modifications of a settlement. A settlement proposal might be accepted by an agency *subject to conditions* which alter or add to the parties' agreement. From the agency's perspective, the changes may be needed to satisfy the statutory standards (*e.g.*, the "public interest") and to protect members of the public who are not represented in a given proceeding. For example, a proposed licensing settlement, which would authorize construction of a utility plant adjacent to a river, might be accepted subject to agency-imposed environmental conditions designed to prevent water pollution. While that might be eminently reasonable, it might also raise construction or operating costs in a way that alters the economics of the utility's settlement bargain.

To protect their bargain from unacceptable changes, the parties' settlement needs to include language which renders the settlement offer void and privileged if agency-required modifications are not subsequently endorsed by the parties. If the modifications are not acceptable to the parties, they need to be able to insist that the agency complete the proceedings which the settlement sought to resolve.

Non-unanimous settlements. The concept of a "non-unanimous" or "contested" settlement might seem bizarre in the context of civil litigation between two or three parties, but it is a very real possibility in some administrative proceedings involving multiple parties and multiple issues. Settlements are often proposed to agencies in multi-party proceedings in which some parties support the settlements terms, but others oppose it. An agency may even find itself facing competing settlement proposals.

Depending on the mix of issues and parties, agencies may take different approaches to a contested settlement proposal.

Decision on the merits. The agency might simply decide the case on the merits based upon a record that adequately addresses the disputed issues. For example, assume that a majority of parties to a power-plant licensing proceeding were to propose a settlement compromising *their* differences (*e.g.*, cost issues) in a manner that is totally unacceptable to other parties (*e.g.*, those concerned with environmental impacts). Here, the results would be zero-sum: the benefits would go to one group; the harms would go to another. There, the agency would have to decide the merits of the contested settlement in light of the applicable statutory and regulatory framework. In the end, it could reject the settlement; or it could accept the settlement subject to modifications acceptable to the parties; or it could propose to accept the settlement as to some issues while requiring further litigation of issues reserved by the agency.

Approval as to some parties. A very different example might be presented in a utility rate-case, in which some parties support the settlement rates, while others oppose the settlement rates they would face. Here, the utility and other settling parties might be willing to "carve out" the dissenters — *i.e.*, settle rate levels for the majority of participants, while the utility and the dissenters would continue to litigate over the rates to be charged to the dissenters. The agency could accept the settlement for some parties and, after litigation, issue a "merits" decision on the remaining disputed rates. In such a case, the utility would gamble that the benefits achieved from settling with most of its customers would outweigh the smaller risks posed by the outliers (*e.g.*, because their litigation budgets are small or their impacts would be low even if they prevailed).

On one hand, gains to the settling parties would not come at the expense of the legal rights of the dissenters, which would be able to continue to litigate for a reasonable rate. Also, this approach has the benefit of protecting settling parties from a "spoiler" who seeks to extract unreasonable concessions by threatening to kill a settlement. On the other hand, this is not as balanced a resolution as it may seem. The reality is that the costs of litigating a rate case are high and small customers would have difficulty protecting their interests in the face of the utility's superior resources.

Confidentiality of negotiations. Confidentiality is obviously critical to settlement negotiations. Parties will be reluctant to discuss compromises below their litigating position if there is a risk that their statements will be held against them. Consequently, settlement procedures are generally treated as confidential, and all proposals are deemed privileged if they are not accepted in full. It is essential that any settlement document explicitly affirm the privileged nature of the offer if it is rejected.[1]

Role of agency staff. To the extent the agency's staff members participate as advocates in a proceeding, they will presumably carry that role forward in negotiations. That is, they will seek to represent the public interest and attempt to assure that a final settlement complies with agency regulations and policies during the negotiations. For settlement discussions to be frank, parties will want assurances that the staff will preserve the confidentiality of the settlement discussions and only comment to the agency on the terms of the final settlement proposal if one is submitted.

---

[1] A special problem may be raised by data shared during settlement discussions. Presumably, data is factual, not merely a matter of position. If a utility shares operating cost or risk data in an effort to persuade parties to agree to a settlement, should the parties be barred from revealing that data to the agency in the litigation if settlement talks fail? Presumably, the public interest requires that decisions be based upon accurate data. Would the utility have any basis for objecting to another party's making such data known to the agency?

EXERCISE 4A — DESIGN AND DRAFT A SETTLEMENT PROPOSAL

Think back to the Homersville bypass problem. There, FERC faces a certificate (licensing) proceeding involving an applicant for authority to construct facilities (North Central) and several intervenors. The intervenors are (a) North Central's potential new customer (Fantastic Manufacturing), which supports the application; (b) Homersville, which would lose its largest customer, be stuck with an unnecessarily large long-term contract, and suffer harm to its bird sanctuary; (c) three groups interested in protecting the town's bird sanctuary (the Homersville Audubon Society, IBU, and the Homersville Taxpayers Alliance, which is also concerned about cost impacts); and (d) the potentially competing pipeline company (Mid-Central Pipeline).

Obviously, no party can get an agreement that achieves all of its objectives. Here is a reminder of the parties' interests.

North Central wants to obtain a certificate to serve Fantastic while still protecting the five-year contract extension with Homersville. That way, it can charge *both* Fantastic and Homersville for transportation that is really needed *only* to serve Fantastic. If it fails to get the certificate or has to give contract relief to Homersville, it will not gain any revenues above its current charges to Homersville. However, Fantastic is concerned that FERC may be persuaded to give Homersville contract relief. It is also concerned that FERC will kill or re-route the project to protect the bird sanctuary.

Fantastic wants the cheapest natural gas possible and eliminating Homersville from its supply chain with an inexpensive bypass would achieve that. It is concerned that the bird sanctuary may kill the proposal or force a re-route that makes the bypass prohibitively expensive. It wonders whether a minor re-route along the outer edge of the bird sanctuary might keep costs in line even as it mitigates harm to the sanctuary to a level acceptable to other parties. It also wonders whether it has enough leverage from the threat of a bypass to get rate concessions from Homersville. Losing the bypass case would take away the leverage.

Homersville wants to kill the bypass, but knows that FERC's policies generally permit bypasses. The bird sanctuary, which Homersville wants to protect, may be the key to blocking the bypass or making it prohibitively expensive. If the bypass cannot be killed, Homersville wants to mitigate North Central's harm to the bird sanctuary and reduce its contract by the amount of direct transportation service that North Central will supply to Fantastic. Fantastic is mostly interested in reducing its costs. Perhaps a local rate concession by Homersville could persuade Fantastic to abandon the bypass.

The Homersville Audubon Society and the International Birders Union want to protect the bird sanctuary.

The Homersville Taxpayers Alliance wants to protect the sanctuary and get contract relief for Homersville.

Mid-Central Pipeline wants to supply Fantastic in place of North Central and Homersville. Its higher costs are less attractive to Fantastic than North Central's, but if it can beat North Central now, perhaps it will have a chance to strike a deal with Fantastic (or even Homersville) in the future.

So here are your tasks.

1. Can you conceive of any set of proposals which might produce a unanimous settlement? Or, if not, what might be the best settlement strategy for Homersville?

2. Using a sample settlement as a model (on the **LEXISNEXIS WEBCOURSE**) draft a settlement proposal on behalf of Homersville, the Homersville Audubon Society, IBU, and the Homersville Taxpayers Alliance which you think might get approved and still achieve all or most of Homersville's objectives. Be sure to include language that protects the parties' deal from modification by FERC. Do this even if you do not believe that a settlement offer is likely to succeed.

Chapter 5

EX PARTE COMMUNICATIONS

ESTIMATED TIME FOR COMPLETION: 60 minutes

ESTIMATED LEVEL OF DIFFICULTY: Moderate

An ongoing issue for administrative proceedings is the extent to which individual entities or their allies are permitted to discuss the substance of contested proceedings with agency decision makers or their advisors, outside the presence of other parties. *Ex parte* communications are generally prohibited in judicial proceedings because they unfairly deny excluded parties the opportunity to know and reply to opposing evidence and influence. Excluding important inputs from the decisional record also undermines public confidence and judicial review. Although agencies often address disputes affecting discrete parties, their mandates are generally broader. Administrative agencies exist to administer laws, and their staffs need flows of information from many sources to do their job well. Consequently, *ex parte* communications may or may not be prohibited in administrative proceedings.

EXERCISE 5A — ADVISING A CLIENT

In the course of your meeting with him, Mr. Marshall of Homersville's natural gas utility, mentions to you that he had learned from Mr. Tom Clark, an official at Fantastic Manufacturing, that lawyers and officers of Fantastic and North Central had met with "senior FERC staff members" two weeks prior to North Central's filing its application for a certificate of public convenience and necessity. Mr. Clark said that their meeting had gone well. He said that they told the staff how much Fantastic hoped to save each year; how the savings could help the company boost profitability and maybe jobs at one of its manufacturing plants; and how the proposal fit within FERC's bypass policies. He said the staff had made some suggestions about what information to include in the application in order to expedite processing.

Mr. Marshall asked Mr. Clark if they had informed the FERC staff about the potential harms to Homersville and its customers or made any mention of the construction in a bird sanctuary. Mr. Clark said they had not. When the staff representatives had asked if there would be opposition, North Central's lawyer said they did not know, but it was "possible." Mr. Clark said he could not remember who the staff representatives were, but North Central had said they included the Director of Pipeline Regulation and senior representatives from several offices which would advise the Commissioners. After the meeting, North Central's lawyer told Mr. Clark that getting approval of the certificate to do the bypass "shouldn't be a problem." Sensing Mr. Marshall's annoyance, Mr. Clark got defensive and would not disclose anything else about the meeting with the agency staff.

Mr. Marshall is angry that the meeting occurred with senior FERC personnel without Homersville being invited. "That just isn't fair. I'll bet they filled the staff's heads with a lot of misleading junk. They sure didn't give the staff our side of the story."

He asks whether Homersville can meet with the FERC Commissioners or the senior staff to present its side of the story. That would only be fair, he asserts. Why should the other side be able to get away with such contacts?

"Even better," he says, "Bobby Roberts, an aide to the Congressman for the Homersville area, is a close friend and former college roommate of FERC's Director of Pipeline Regulation, who will be involved in the decision." Bobby is scheduled to take his friend to a D.C. steakhouse for dinner to talk about old times. Bobby has invited Mr. Marshall to come along. He says it would be a great opportunity to talk about the case. Bobby adds, "Even if you can't make it, you can let me know the details, and I'll fill him in on the problems the proposal would cause Homersville."

As you know, FERC has published a notice of the proceeding to review North Central's application and it has invited interventions and protests. You also know that Homersville intends to file an intervention and protest raising a number of issues and asking for a formal hearing. You expect other intervenors to do the same.

Look at the APA and FERC's *ex parte* rules (on the **LEXISNEXIS WEBCOURSE**), particularly the highlighted sections. Prepare a short memo or letter advising Mr. Marshall about the *ex parte* contact limitations applicable to the proceeding.

(a)   Is there anything wrong with the pre-filing meeting between North Central and the Staff?

(b)   Would you advise Homersville to try to arrange a meeting with the FERC staff to discuss the issues either before or after its protest and request for hearing has been filed?

(c)   How would you advise him concerning the congressional aide's dinner invitation? Why?

In thinking about your advice, you should consider more than just whether the contacts would be lawful. There is also the question whether making an *ex parte* contact would be prudent? You need to consider all the possible benefits and downsides from making such an approach. For example, could the decision maker be made to look bad or forced to recuse himself? Might a questionable contact cause an agency officer to bend over backwards not to appear to be inappropriately influenced. Are there potential sanctions if your advice is wrong? Would you or your client would be embarrassed if your actions appeared on the front page of a newspaper or on a popular blog. How much influence will your client gain from an *ex parte* contact and will the potential gain outweigh the risks?

(Note that in Part 4 — Open Government, there is an exercise raising the issue of how the Freedom of Information Act might be brought to bear in addressing Mr. Marshall's concerns.)

PART TWO

OVERVIEW

Agencies not only decide particularized disputes, they also make and implement policy. Agencies typically have choices on how to develop those policies. Policies can be made on a case-by-case basis through adjudications or they can be promulgated through rules and regulations.

The choice between rulemaking and adjudication to develop policy invokes practical considerations of notice, fairness, and efficiency. Promulgation of policies through regulations has a clear advantage in the realm of efficiency. Rules can be promulgated for an entire industry in a single public proceeding. Typically, the rules will be based on an informal, notice-and-comment proceeding in which all interested persons are free to submit comments and may be invited to make an oral presentation as well.[1]

Assuming they are well written, the resulting rules will provide clear notice to affected companies and individuals as to what is required of them in the future. To be sure, some ambiguities will remain to be resolved when the rules are applied in individual cases, but the broad rules should be relatively clear from a regulation. The "concise general statement of their basis and purpose" contained in the preambles to the orders promulgating those regulations will provide further guidance on the purpose and operation of the rules. There should be less need to guess about the meaning of prior precedents and fewer worries about whether one has overlooked a precedent. Implementing policies through regulations also has an important element

---

[1] Section 553 of the APA (5 U.S.C. § 553) sets the procedures for informal rulemaking in federal agency proceedings. Sections 556 and 557 (5 U.S.C. §§ 556–557) set forth additional procedural requirements for formal adjudications.

of fairness: everyone in an industry knows that it and its competitors are subject to the same rules which everyone can read.

By contrast, use of adjudication to develop policies requires case-by-case review and a gradual development of precedent. It allows particularized solutions within an evolving framework of statutory interpretation and policy decisions. However, while some parties may feel that adjudications afford them the fairness of a full hearing of their special arguments and circumstances, others will complain about having to operate without clear prior guidance as to what is permitted and what is prohibited when a new situation is potentially distinguishable from prior cases. Not only is precedent less subject to reliance until your client's specific facts have been heard and compared to earlier decisions, but precedent can be modified based on new circumstances presented in your client's case.

Case-by-case review is also more costly and less efficient than policy development through one or a few rulemaking proceedings. While full participation in a rulemaking may not be cheap, it will almost certainly be more expensive for every member of an industry to seek adjudications every time they want a ruling on a regulatory issue.

Courts, of course, make policy through adjudication, and the common law is based on incremental change in the face of evolving factual contexts. That is in the nature of courts: they decide individual cases; they do not have the power to promulgate general rules.

Normally, however, when we think of policy making, we think of the legislature and the passage of new statutes. Legislators are elected officials and accountability for their decisions is at the ballot box. Moreover, as politicians they are expected to meet with a wide variety of constituents and entertain a host of possible policy outcomes.

Agency directors or commissioners, however, are not elected. Agency heads or commissioners usually are appointed by the President of the United States with advice and consent of the Senate or by the Governor of a State, possibly subject to confirmation by the legislature. The same legislature establishes the limits of the agency's authority, the applicable policies and standards to be applied, the scope of actions the agency can take, and the general forms of the procedures to be employed. The legislature also controls the funding of the agency, which can directly or indirectly affect policy and procedural choices made by the agency over time.

Moreover, when they are making policy in a rulemaking context as opposed to an adjudicatory proceeding, the Due Process Clause usually does not apply to such proceedings. The decisions rendered are not based on individualized factual scenarios; they are generally applicable policy determinations that are based on broad findings, which are usually generally applicable, and not particular to any one individual.

When an agency promulgates a rule, that rule must be authorized by the statute under which it operates. We will explore just what this means more fully when we look at judicial review of agency actions in Part 3. Courts will, under certain circumstances, defer to an agency's interpretation of its own statute when making such determinations.

Assuming the agency has the statutory authority to make the rules it plans to promulgate, how does it do that? As we will see, one way is to issue a rule pursuant to the Administrative Procedure Act. Section 553 governs informal rulemaking and it requires simple notice of the proposed rule and an opportunity for interested persons to comment by way of "written data, views, or arguments with or without opportunity for oral presentation." Unlike the formal adjudicatory provisions of the APA, set forth in sections 554, 556 and 557 (which also apply to formal rulemaking proceedings whenever rules are required by statute to be made on the record), this provision does not say anything about *ex parte* contacts nor does it explicitly require a rulemaking record. It does require that final rules be accompanied by a concise statement of basis and purpose. Section 553 also provides for a host of exemptions from its processes in various contexts such as the military or when contracts are involved. Various forms of policy making are also exempt including interpretive rules, policy statements, or rules of agency organization or procedure.

The APA is not the only statute that might be involved when a federal agency makes policy. The agency's own enabling act may describe additional or alternative procedures to be used for a rulemaking proceeding. These processes may set forth what are called hybrid rulemaking procedures — processes that combine aspects of adjudication along with policy making processes. Many environmental, health and safety rules are made with these more extensive procedures.

Beyond statutes that specifically dictate the substantive policy framework within which the agency must act, Congress also has passed various statutes that seek to regulate the impact of rules on certain interests which cut across substantive areas. Examples of these cross-cutting statutes include the Regulatory Flexibility Act (5 U.S.C. § 601), the Paperwork Reduction Act (44 U.S.C. § 3501) and the National Environmental Policy Act (42 U.S.C. § 4321 *et seq.*).

Rulemakings typically begin with a notice of proposed rulemaking (NOPR). The notice is expected to describe the proposed rule, the reasons for the proposed rule (the statutory basis, nature of the problems to be addressed, the factual basis for the agency's concern, and how the proposed rule will address the problems), and the specific regulations to be codified. The notice will also describe how and when members of the public may submit comments on the proposed rule.

In some instances, agencies will start the public-input process with a more open-ended "notice of inquiry" or an "advanced notice of proposed rulemaking" or another pre-rulemaking process, in which the agency identifies an area of policy concern, broadly describes possible policy options, and solicits public input on the direction it should take. The result of the pre-rulemaking process is a better informed rulemaking proposal, which anticipates the public's thinking about the issues to be addressed.

The exercises that follow seek to acquaint you with some of the considerations that help determine whether to use rulemaking or adjudicative procedures in the first instance as well as basic skills required in rulemaking processes.

Chapter 6

THE CHOICE BETWEEN RULEMAKING AND ADJUDICATION

ESTIMATED TIME FOR COMPLETION: 45 minutes

ESTIMATED LEVEL OF DIFFICULTY: Moderate

The purpose of this problem is to reconstruct the litigation strategies and theories of the parties involved in the *Vermont Yankee* litigation. This case should be in your casebook; it is also online. The purpose of this exercise is to enable you to think through the relationships of rulemaking procedures to adjudicatory procedures as well as some of the strategies that underlie the advocacy of one approach to decision making over another.

The following exercise provides an opportunity to study these relationships from the various points of view of different litigants and to assess their legality and strategic interest. In so doing, you will be able to reconstruct or re-engineer the strategies and decisions made by the litigants in the *Vermont Yankee* case, by formulating and assessing the litigation strategies that most likely underlie the approaches to this case taken by the utility involved, the environmental groups which intervened, and the Nuclear Regulatory Commission. To further this goal, we suggest that the class be divided into three groups — one group represents the utility; another group represents the environmentalists; and one group plays the role of attorneys for the Nuclear Regulatory Commission.

EXERCISE 6 — VERMONT YANKEE STRATEGIES

(1)   As the attorney for Vermont Yankee, what are your primary goals in this litigation? What do you think of the agency's decision to use informal rulemaking procedures to resolve the issue of nuclear waste? What advantages and what disadvantages do you see in this manner of proceeding? What kind of record will you want to develop? Will it withstand judicial review?

(2)   As the attorney for NRDC, what are your primary goals in this litigation? What are your views on the agency's decision to resolve the nuclear waste issue through informal rulemaking? Why do you wish to resist this procedure? What kind of hearing do you envisage? Why do you want that kind of hearing? Is your primary audience the agency or the court or the public? How important is delay to you? What is the impact of delay? Are there ethical limits to the use of the litigation process to effectuate delay? Do you have reasons, independent of delay, for the procedures you advocate? What are they?

(3)   As the attorney for the Nuclear Regulatory Commission, what are your primary goals? Why did you recommend the use of informal rulemaking procedures? What are you trying to accomplish with these procedures? Are these procedures fair? Why did you augment them? Why did you resist augmenting them further?

Chapter 7

HOW TO FIND RULEMAKING PROCEEDINGS AND FILE COMMENTS

ESTIMATED TIME FOR COMPLETION: 45 minutes

ESTIMATED LEVEL OF DIFFICULTY: Easy

Agencies are not free to manufacture regulations out of thin air (though they are sometimes accused of doing so). The Administrative Procedure Act and, in some instances, the relevant substantive statutes prescribe procedures for promulgating regulations.

This chapter will have you dig into the mechanics of the rulemaking process, exploring the process by which federal agencies promulgate regulations, how you can track down rulemakings for your clients, and how you can submit comments on behalf of your clients.

When a client contacts you for help participating in a rulemaking, he likely will only have partial information about the proceeding. He may have read about a proposal in a newspaper or trade publication or heard about it from a colleague. He may not know much more than that an agency has made a proposal which could affect his business (or important interests that his non-profit group seeks to defend). If you are lucky, he will know the agency and when the rulemaking was initiated. If you are *very* lucky, he will already know the docket number. More likely, he will know the topic, the potential impact, maybe how recently it was issued, and perhaps the agency. In any event, he will expect you to find out more about the proposal and advise him on what he can do to advance it, change it, or stop it.[1]

---

[1] If you are a regular practitioner in a regulatory field, you are likely to be the one initiating the conversation. Keeping clients informed of regulatory developments is an important part of practicing administrative law. Not only do clients welcome timely information about proposals that may affect them, but updating clients is a valuable business development tool.

Your first task will be to find the proceeding, figure out its procedural status (*e.g.*, whether the comment period is still open), evaluate the notice of proposed rulemaking (or rule if it has been issued already), and figure out what the client can do to protect his or her interests.

As you will discover from the following exercise, some agencies' proceedings are easier to locate than others. For example, the Federal Energy Regulatory Commission has a user-friendly website that you can easily navigate to find rulemaking proceedings and documents. Often, other agencies' proposals are not as easy to find. Fortunately, www.regulations.gov provides a centralized location to search for proceedings across many — but not all — federal agencies. The Federal Register is the official publication for notices and rules issued by federal agencies. It is particularly important since comment periods are often defined as a specified number of days from publication of a notice in the Federal Register.

EXERCISE 7A — FINDING RULEMAKING NOTICES AND RECORDS

For the sake of illustration, find a notice of proposed rulemaking and a final rule issued by FERC in rulemaking dockets during the past year. Start with the website of the Federal Energy Regulatory Commission at www.ferc.gov. Go to "Documents and Filings"; then to "eLibrary"; then to "General Search." In "General Search," pick a date range covering the past three years. Select "Issuances," and, in the "Docket Number" box, type the letters "RM" (which is the standard prefix for all FERC rulemaking dockets). Hit "Submit." Review the results of your search. You should find rulemaking notices, orders, and statements by individual commissioners, press releases, and a few other types of documents.

Now, from that set of results choose a final rule and look at the rulemaking order. First, identify the docket number and determine when the proceeding was initiated by a notice of proposed rulemaking. Next, look over the order to see its organization and structure. Among other things, look at how the order sets forth the rule's purpose; the issues being addressed; the comments received; how the agency responds to the comments; how the final regulations are set forth; and the formal issues addressed toward the end of the order.

Now use the docket number for the final rule you selected and the issuance date for the original notice of proposed rulemaking to initiate a new search with the "General Search" tool in order to locate the docket sheet, the original notice of proposed rulemaking ("NOPR"), and all the documents filed in that rulemaking docket. To get the docket sheet, you will need to click both "Issuances" and "Submittals" under the heading "category" of document. [Note that for a manageably sized rulemaking proceeding, you might try Docket No. RM11-15.]

Once the docket sheet comes up, look at the Notice of Proposed Rulemaking to see how it is structured and the procedures it describes for submitting comments. Look at two or three examples of comments filed by entities interested enough in the rulemaking to file comments. Again, get an idea of how they prepared their comments, both the formal structure of their comments and the way they structured their argument.

EXERCISE 7B — REGULATIONS.GOV

Regulations.gov is a useful website for finding federal rulemakings and, in many cases, for tracking and participating in rulemaking proceedings. However, you should be aware that not all agencies participate in Regulations.gov, as explained on the FAQ page of the website.

The best way to understand it is to use Regulations.gov to find a rule or rulemaking proceeding.

For information about how to use Regulations.gov, review the

The FAQ page: http://www.regulations.gov/#!faqs

The Help page tutorial: http://www.regulations.gov/#!help

The Glossary: http://www.regulations.gov/#!glossary

Then, go to www.regulations.gov and use the search feature to experiment with how it works. Pick a period of time and two or three agencies of interest. Look to see what rulemaking orders were issued in that period and then pick one or two and find the comments that were submitted.

If you find an open rulemaking of interest, sign up for email alerts which will allow you to track the rulemaking's progress and eventual outcome.

The following are examples of recent rulemakings you might try if you do not have any luck with pure experimentation:

http://www.regulations.gov/#!documentDetail;D=DOT-OST-2011-0044-0003 — prohibiting electric cigarettes on aircraft

http://www.regulations.gov/#!documentDetail;D=CIA-2011-0002-0001   — CIA amendments to its FOIA rules

http://www.regulations.gov/#!documentDetail;D=EPA-HQ-SFUND-2011-0647-0001 — EPA Priorities List

http://www.regulations.gov/#!documentDetail;D=FWS-R4-ES-2010-0024-0021 — Endangered Species Act

http://www.regulations.gov/#!documentDetail;D=CPSC-2011-0074-0001   — CPSC Saw Stop Advanced Notice of Proposed Rulemaking

EXERCISE 7C — STATE ADMINISTRATIVE PROCEEDINGS

Experiment with finding a state administrative rulemaking proceeding. Explore the website of agency websites in your home State or the State where you may hope to practice law. Websites of state public utility or public service commissions often provide good examples.

Spend a few minutes trying to find a rulemaking proceeding initiated or concluded by an agency in the last two years. Find a notice of proposed rulemaking and any final order. See if you can find copies of the comments filed by parties. Can you locate the agency's existing regulations?

Depending upon the State and the agency, the information available online may be limited. You may need to look at more than one agency's website in order to find one that gives you a useful example. Still, the exercise of trying to locate agency documents provides useful experience with how to find information that you will need to obtain once you are practicing law.

Exchange your findings with others in your class in order to get a broader sample of the state administrative resources you can find online.

Chapter 8

DEVELOPING A RULEMAKING STRATEGY.

ESTIMATED TIME FOR COMPLETION: 90 minutes

ESTIMATED LEVEL OF DIFFICULTY: Difficult

There are several key issues to consider in approaching a rulemaking proposal for an interested client. In thinking about these issues, you need to view the issues from the perspectives of the agency and the public, as well as your client's perspective. You also need to anticipate the comments likely to be filed by other potential participants, whether you view them as allies or opponents.

Remember that the agency is trying to satisfy statutory standards and policies set by the legislature, and it is trying to advance the public interest as it sees it. Its view of the public interest may be very different from your client's, but you need to understand it if you want to increase your chances of influencing the agency. Thus, when contemplating commenting on an agency's proposal, you need to "put on the agency's glasses" to see the world as it sees it, and you need to employ its language in your comments. Make your comments respectful and constructive. If you fail to do so, your chances of persuading the agency are likely to be dramatically reduced.

Substantive analysis

The first issues you must consider are substantive and contextual. An agency wants to achieve specified goals and generally wants to get there with as little collateral damage as possible. With that in mind, consider the following questions along with your client's concerns:

What has the agency proposed and has it supported its proposal?

-   What does the proposal intend to accomplish and how will it work?

-   What does it replace or amend?

-   Has the agency reasonably described and supported the proposal?

59

- Is the proposal procedurally and substantively consistent with the underlying statute and other relevant statutes?

- Has the agency correctly assessed the potential costs and benefits of its proposal?

- How would the proposal affect your client (*e.g.*, compliance costs, impacts on business practices and outlook)?

- How would the proposal affect the rest of the public?

- Will it have unintended side-effects?

- Can the rulemaking proposal be modified to ameliorate adverse impacts on your client and the public?

- Can the rulemaking proposal be modified to *improve* its effectiveness while reducing the impacts on your client or the public?

Does your client want to support, oppose, or modify the proposed rule?

- Does your client have in-house expertise to support its comment, or will it need expert help?

- Does it want to participate directly or through an organization, such as a trade association?

Your client will presumably be the best source of information concerning the commercial and technological environment in which it operates, and therefore it will be in the best position to assess the impacts of a rule on its business. Depending on the nature of the proposal, you and your client may need to bring in experts in science, engineering, economics, or other fields fully to assess and comment on the pros and cons of a rulemaking proposal.

However, lawyers can bring important, independent perspectives to the substantive analysis of a rulemaking proposal. In all likelihood, the client will look to its lawyer, at a minimum, for guidance on how the proposed rule will operate; how it will fit within the broader context of existing laws and regulations; what the prospects are for achieving a given change; ethical limitations on possible arguments and strategies; and, procedurally, how to file comments and persuade the relevant agency. The client will also look to its lawyer for guidance on the prospects for achieving its objectives through judicial review, if it cannot achieve its goals at the agency level. The client may also look to its lawyer for guidance on how the other potential players are likely to approach the rulemaking. The latter question is important for identifying potential issues, allies and opponents, which can be critical for implementing an effective rulemaking strategy. For these reasons, lawyers often specialize in certain areas of regulation. The expertise they develop is substantive as well as legal and procedural.

Strategic Issues

Once you have a clear sense of what the proposal would do and how it would affect your client, the next issues are strategic — how can you persuade the agency to make the changes your client desires. That must be your first goal. If you lose at the agency level, you will fight an uphill battle against the deference courts pay to an agency's findings and interpretations.

Your comments should try to strike a balance between legal and policy arguments. If you have a strong argument that an agency proposal, if adopted, would exceed the agency's authority, then hit it hard and lay the groundwork for judicial review. However, unless the legal argument is a sure winner, do not stop there. Agencies are obviously attuned to legal arguments, since they have a cadre of lawyers, and they do not want to be reversed or otherwise embarrassed. But they are ultimately interested in achieving policy objectives within the boundaries permitted by applicable statutes and their other policies. Indeed, the boundaries of permissible agency action can be shaped by the statute's policy objectives — broad policies may beget broad flexibility in designing an agency's remedies. You will not advance your client's cause by dwelling on hyper-technical legal arguments, and giving short shrift to the proposal's policy and practical implications. Conversely, you will enhance your cause if you can present credible factual information, strong technical analysis and reasoned arguments for modifying a proposal, particularly if your proposed modifications will still enable the agency to achieve its central goals.

Even on appeal, if all the policy arguments are on the agency's side, courts are more likely to defer to an agency's legal judgments and regulatory choices. On the other hand, an agency's failure to grapple with commenters' factual and policy arguments will significantly increase your chances of getting a reversal or remand for further consideration. Despite contrary protestations, judges do care about policy arguments. You are more likely to persuade a judge that the agency's legal or policy analysis is unreasonable if you can persuade him or her that it produces an unreasonable result or is out of sync with the *factual* record you have helped develop.

With those considerations in mind, consider the following questions in connection with a rulemaking proposal you are asked to comment on:

When are comments due and will there be a rulemaking hearing?

What are your client's concerns and what changes to the proposed rule might allay its concerns?

- Do you need to undertake an all-out assault on the proposal as being inconsistent with the statute or the public interest (assuming that is even a credible option)?

- Can you portray your proposed modifications as a "tweak" or as addressing a niche problem, which will alleviate your client's potential difficulties without undermining the agency's substantive objectives?

- Can you *help* the agency achieve its desired outcome more effectively while still mitigating your client's problems?

What legal, policy, and factual arguments can you make that might move the final rule in your client's direction?

- Has the agency complied with the APA and any other applicable procedures for conducting a rulemaking?

- Does its NOPR adequately explain the proposal and its basis?

- Has it complied with its other statutory obligations, such as an environmental or paperwork impact statement?

- How should you approach the rulemaking? Should your comments be long and detailed, or are you better off with shorter, targeted comments?

- Can you help your cause by providing technical data and arguments?

- Would your arguments be materially strengthened by affidavits or an expert's report?

- Can you propose specific regulatory language?

- How will other interested entities comment on the proposal and how should your strategy anticipate their involvement?

- Should you or your client make an oral presentation if there is a rulemaking hearing?

Assuming direct approaches are possible (legally and within the agency's culture), can you profitably approach an influential official with information, questions, and arguments?

Do you need to lay the groundwork for judicial review and, if so, how does that affect your strategy for building a record?

- Unless the matter is such that your client will never consider going to court, you should approach the rulemaking with the idea of creating a record that may allow you to succeed on judicial review.

- At a minimum, your procedural and substantive objections need to be preserved and you need to lay a factual foundation so your substantive arguments are well supported.

Would your client benefit from pursuing political support from the legislative or the executive branch or from other levels of government?

- If so, how would you go about it?

- What are the politics surrounding the proposal — is it a high-profile, hotly contested proposal, or a lower-priority proposal, which is primarily of interest to industry insiders? What allies could you enlist?

- What are the risks that perceived bullying from the outside (particularly from a minority party) will backfire?

A Very Practical Issue

Once you have understood the proposal and conceived of the comments you will file, you face a very simple, practical question: how do you get your comments noticed and closely read by the agency?

It is probably safe to say that all comments submitted will be glanced at by someone. But that is not enough by itself. You need to have your clients' comments stand out enough to be taken seriously and you need your comments to persuade the agency to make as many of the desired changes as possible.

In a rulemaking with little public interest, the pile of comments will be small, and your client's comments, if well written and constructive, will get serious attention. However, in a major rulemaking in which dozens or perhaps hundreds of comments are filed, the problem of being taken seriously is much more substantial. The agency has only limited staff resources and it will need to prioritize.

Your job will be to get your comments in the "high-priority" pile for close examination. It is safe to say that your comments will get attention if your client is a major trade association or public interest group with a reputation for useful, substantive comments and a history of seeking judicial review. It is also safe to say that your comments will get very little attention if they are vague and resemble the mass emailed comments that are now made possible by the Internet. In between, you face a challenge, which is the subject of the next exercise.

FACTUAL BACKGROUND FOR EXERCISES
8A-8B — AN ENVIRONMENTAL RULEMAKING

The "Federal Emissions Agency" ("FEA") has issued a Notice of Proposed Rulemaking to implement air quality standards under the (hypothetical) "Hazardous Air Pollution Act" ("HAPA") which requires the Administrator to protect air quality from hazardous emissions.

Section 2(a) of HAPA requires the Administrator to establish air quality standards, stating in part:

> Air quality criteria for an air pollutant shall accurately reflect the latest emission data and scientific knowledge useful in indicating the kind and extent of all identifiable effects on public health or welfare which may be expected from the presence of such pollutant in the ambient air, in varying quantities.

Section 2(b)(1) of HAPA provides, in relevant part:

> (1) Simultaneously with the issuance of air quality criteria under subsection (a) of this section, the Administrator shall, after conducting a rulemaking proceeding and consultation with appropriate advisory committees and Federal departments and agencies, issue appropriate standards for air pollution control technologies and techniques to be implemented by stationary sources of hazardous air pollutants. Such standards shall require implementation of the best available control technologies or operating measures or some combination of technologies and techniques designed to reduce hazardous air pollutants to levels that satisfy the air quality criteria established by the Administrator as expeditiously as reasonably practicable.

And, HAPA Section 2 (b)(4) states:

> (4) The Administrator shall promulgate rules requiring regular monitoring and submission of pollution emissions data by stationary sources as appropriate to implement the purposes of this Act.

The NOPR proposes to require all manufacturers that emit more than 10 tons of Methyloxystuff during any "12-month period" to implement the "best available technology" ("BACT") within two years of crossing the emissions threshold of 10 tons in any 12-month period. The NOPR states that the measurement period is a "rolling" twelve months. The rulemaking proposal cites and describes a dozen epidemiological and laboratory studies published within the past 10 years which show that Methyloxystuff is a carcinogen that does not disperse well when emitted from smokestacks. Atmospheric emissions of Methyloxystuff are entirely the product of manufacturing "phlogistia," a specialty chemical used in a variety of industrial processes, including manufacturing certain agricultural chemicals. The NOPR would also require all sources of Methyloxystuff to submit detailed annual and quarterly reports of their emissions of Methyloxystuff for each month and peak day, to provide monthly air quality samples at specified distances from the sources, and to report any workplace exposures to the chemical.

Wanda Knight, the general counsel of your client, Chemicals Galore, LLC, says she is appalled. She tells you that the "Best Available Control Technology" is really expensive. Installing BACT in a 15-year old, small manufacturing facility like the one they operate would eliminate the company's potential profits on that plant for four or five years. She says that she isn't sure the plant could stay in business if the company had to install and operate that equipment. "Maybe a BACT requirement makes sense for one of the big manufacturers," she says, "but not for a little plant like Chemicals Galore operates." The company's plants for making other chemicals "are not profitable enough to make up for those costs," she asserts.

Ms. Knight acknowledges that Chemicals Galore emits Methyloxystuff as a byproduct of making phlogistia. In the last ten years, her firm has exceeded the 10-ton level in at least five rolling twelve-month periods, but it has only exceeded the proposed 10-ton limit once in a calendar year and that could have been avoided.

She explains that manufacturing phlogistia is cyclical business. When the industry's customers are doing well, the demand for the chemical is high. Sixty percent or more of Chemical Galore's annual production is likely to occur in one or two months, typically in the Spring, and then drop off. If two high-production periods occur within 12 months of each other (*e.g.*, in April-May of one year and February-March of the next), the company can easily exceed the 10-ton limit in a rolling 12-month period. This has happened frequently in the last ten years. Ms. Knight explains that the company needs to satisfy orders out of its own production in the high-demand months because prices and profit margins are highest then.

On the other hand, if the company were only required to stay under the 10-ton emissions limit on a *calendar year* basis, it could manage its production in a way that stays under the 10-ton annual target and still remain profitable. That is, if it has a late-Spring manufacturing peak, it would shift, during a few off-peak months, from *producing* phlogistia to *purchasing* phlogistia to meet its orders. Since phlogistia prices are low in off-peak periods and the big manufacturers will continue to operate, Chemicals Galore could buy and resell phlogistia to keep its customers happy while continuing to make an annual profit and never installing BACT emissions technology. Since the big producers will have to install BACT, she says, buying from them in off-peak periods would mitigate Methyloxystuff emissions for that portion of her company's phlogistia sales.

Ms. Knight says she has doubts about the FEA's health studies. She has had employees inhale higher concentrations of Methyloxystuff in the course of their work than the public would breath. Apart from those who also smoked cigarettes, she doesn't recall their getting cancer at any unusual rate, though some have had shortness-of-breath issues. There was a Congressman from Louisiana who breathed a whole jar of what he said was Methyloxystuff on the House floor just to prove it was safe. He lost the next election, but, as far as she knows, he's still alive.

In response to your questions, Ms. Knight tells you:

- The studies cited by the agency indicate a 60% increase in lung cancer rates within 50 miles of phlogistia plants. But, she says that the national background rates for lung cancer among non-smokers are low, so *she* isn't worried about cancer rates increasing from Methyloxystuff with or without BACT.

- Chemicals Galore is a member of a trade association, the National Association of Phlogistia Manufacturers, and a national chemical trade association. She understands that each of the associations is planning to submit comments with a study to show that Methyloxystuff is not as bad as the other studies suggest. The study is by a chemical industry consulting firm which specializes in disputing health-impact allegations. There are three other small manufacturers of phlogistia. She does not know for sure, but they might be similarly situated in terms of production levels and emissions. On the other hand, she does not want to share their strategy for buying phlogistia in low-price periods since that could drive up the price and may raise competition issues — "Not that they won't figure it out on their own soon enough."

- Her engineers say Chemicals Galore would probably incur $20 million to install "hyper-scrubbers" which is the most likely approved BACT since it is commercially available technology that reduces Methyloxystuff emissions by 90%. Annual scrubber operating, maintenance and disposal costs would be about $2 million per year. A second emissions technology option, water-based scrubbers, would cost about $5 million, but it is only half as effective removing Methyloxystuff from a plant's emissions. Either way, the new equipment would last 15–20 years, and would probably be depreciated in five to seven years.

- Reporting issues, she says, are also a concern. The reporting requirement proposed by the agency would require installation of monitoring equipment for approximately $1,000,000, a mobile air-sampling unit for $200,000, and perhaps 150 hours of employees' time to assemble and review the annual and quarterly reports. The company already checks the workplace, but she does not want to share that information with anyone. Also, the annual and quarterly reports might draw attention to the Spring emissions peaks, which might attract future regulatory proposals or law suits.

- A significant potential cost from emissions reporting would be the adverse publicity and possible law suits if the emissions data is made public. Already, some plaintiffs' lawyers have been contacted by lung-cancer patients about possibly suing Chemical Galore. Keeping the data confidential should be a goal.

- Chemicals Galore's phlogistia plant employs about 100 workers, and approximately 30 independent truck drivers are kept busy hauling phlogistia. She guesses that 200–300 jobs are directly or indirectly associated with the Chemicals Galore's phlogistia business.

- The last time FEA considered Methyloxystuff, dozens of comments were filed by trade associations, manufacturers, public health organizations, and environmental groups, and hundreds of comments were filed by citizens. She thinks there could be more this time because environmental groups have been lobbying for new regulations.

- Citing concentrated and poorly dispersed emissions, environmental groups have been emphasizing the danger of local "hot spots" of pollution. They are proposing that BACT be required for all plants that emit one ton or more of

Methyloxystuff in any 60-day period. That would clearly affect Chemicals Galore.

With that background, Ms. Knight asks what action you would recommend that Chemicals Galore take in order to head off those regulatory burdens. The company president wants to fight.

EXERCISE 8A: DESIGNING A STRATEGY

When you review the NOPR, you find that she has accurately described the proposed rule and the agency's proposal to treat hyperscrubbers as the best available control technology for covered sources of Methyloxystuff pollution.

The NOPR cites a dozen scientific studies showing that exposure to Methyloxystuff is associated with increased emphysema, asthma, lung cancer, and some childhood development issues. The NOPR proposes to establish air quality criteria setting the maximum ambient level of ground-level Methyloxystuff air pollution at a uniform level which would be exceeded near Chemical Galore's phlogistia plant during peak production periods.

The NOPR proposes a BACT compliance obligation based on a 12-month average emissions level in excess of 10 tons per stationary source. It makes no mention of possible "air pollution . . . techniques" or "operating measures" to limit pollution. Although the NOPR addresses the problem of regional concentrations of Methyloxystuff (within 50 miles of an emissions source), nothing in the rulemaking proposal discusses the issue of seasonal production patterns. Written comments are due within 60 days after the proposal appears in the Federal Register.

Based on what you know and your review of the Hazardous Air Pollution Act, prepare a memorandum outlining your recommended strategy for Chemicals Galore's participation in the FEA's rulemaking proceeding. For purposes of the exercise, assume that the agency has legal authority to promulgate a rule limiting Methyloxystuff and prescribing the appropriate technology or technologies to be used.

1.   What issues would you propose that Chemicals Galore fully address and what issues might it address on a more limited basis?

2.   What would you recommend that Chemicals Galore do in order to maximize the chances that FEA will closely read the comments and address them favorably?

In thinking about Chemicals Galore's comments, would you propose, for example, to:

Raise any challenges to the agency's compliance with the Hazardous Air Pollution Act?

Challenge the underlying health science of Methyloxystuff?

Emphasize economic impacts on small manufacturing plants?

Propose changing the measurement period by shifting the 10-ton emissions trigger to a calendar year emissions from a rolling 12-month emissions level, as proposed by Ms. Knight?

Propose that the agency permit use of the cheaper emissions control technology at least at smaller plants, like your client's?

Propose allowing small plants longer than two years to install the BACT?

Encourage a liberal waiver policy for small companies?

Ask that annual and quarterly reports be kept confidential?

What procedural steps would you recommend to your client and how can you make CG's comments stand out?

Submit written comments?

Call the agency or try to arrange a meeting with key agency personnel?

Coordinate with other manufacturers or the trade associations?

Seek to form a coalition of small manufacturers or have them join Chemicals Galore's comments?

Include studies or affidavits in comments?

Include judicial review language in your comments (*e.g.*, "it would be arbitrary and capricious for the agency to do . . ." or "FEA would exceed its statutory authority if it . . .")?

Participate in oral presentation?

Bring on political pressures?

Implement a full public relations campaign?

Whatever strategies you adopt, remember that it is very important to develop and preserve your credibility and your clients' credibility. This is particularly true for lawyers and clients who regularly appear before an agency, but it is true for all those who appear before a regulator. Regulators do not want to be surprised to find out that they took action based on invalid information and arguments that you supplied. Regulators can have long memories of who made misstatements and misleading arguments. They know you are an advocate, but if they think they have to double check every factual and legal assertion you make, you and your clients will be much worse off.

EXERCISE 8B — DESIGNING A DIFFERENT STRATEGY

Now assume that you represent a coalition of environmental groups that plans to participate in the proceeding.

What would you argue and what would you do to maximize the attention the FEA pays to your clients' comments? Would it be any different from the steps you would recommend that Chemicals Galore take?

Chapter 9

ETHICS IN FILING RULEMAKING COMMENTS

ESTIMATED TIME FOR COMPLETION: 90 minutes

ESTIMATED LEVEL OF DIFFICULTY: Difficult

A question arises as to how far a lawyer can or should go in promoting his client's interests before a regulatory agency. A classic example is the temptation to exaggerate adverse impacts or scientific uncertainties in pursuit of a favorable outcome for a client, even if there is likely to be public harm from delayed regulation. Arguments that exploit "uncertainty" to delay regulations have long been used to preserve harmful industrial practices, such as pollution and cigarette distribution, well after scientific evidence points to a probable — perhaps highly probable — link between the industrial activity and public harm. The tendency to cite "up to" adverse impacts without contextualizing the probabilities can be found on both sides of many regulatory arguments.

In traditional judicial proceedings, the lawyer's obligation to engage in zealous advocacy is well established. It is premised on the view that discovery and the clash of presentations and counter-presentations by the interested parties will enable a jury or judge to ferret out the truth. Cross-examination and discovery help uncover the basis or lack of basis for each party's claims, thereby mitigating the dangers of misleading claims. In most traditional judicial proceedings, the relevant individuals or companies (*e.g.*, the signatories to a disputed contract) are represented, and their interests are fairly easily defined by a complaint and answer or by an indictment and plea. The final decision is made by a neutral party based upon a clearly defined record. Political pressure or *ex parte* communications with the judge or jury would plainly be beyond the pale. Strategies and the range of permissible arguments are fairly tightly controlled by established law rules of procedure and evidence.

In the administrative context, informal rulemaking proceedings are very different. They frequently involve issues that will affect many companies or thousands or even millions of people, many of whom do not participate and may not be actively represented in the proceeding. No strict rules of evidence apply to rulemakings.

Anyone with an interest can participate. Discovery and cross-examination are not available to test the validity of submissions in informal rulemakings. *Ex parte* communications by interested individuals and politicians are permitted. The record of decision is much less precisely defined than in judicial proceedings. In addition to the official record, agency personnel will consider information received *ex parte*, reports that have been prepared by the agency or others, input from other agencies, and political input, especially from within the Administration. In addition, administrative decisions are expected to be based in large part on the agency's expertise, which has been built up based on years of regulation and on analyses undertaken or collected by the agency staff.

An important question for practitioners is how far can they go in their "zealous" advocacy? If the studies they cite and the factual claims they make are not subject to cross-examination or discovery, do advocates have an obligation to disclose conflicting data or weaknesses in their factual claims or studies? While they clearly cannot make false statements, can they ethically make exaggerated or misleading claims in a rulemaking proceeding? Should they show restraint in the claims and arguments they make? If a lawyer says that a proposed rule would create great technical difficulty for her client, should she have more than just the client's unquestioned assertion as a basis for making the claim? Suppose she asks the corporate client for the details and learns: "well, there could be some additional maintenance a couple times a year and the cost would be a few thousand dollars each time." How far can she go in painting a picture of a heavy burden, as the client wants? Does she need to disclose the details knowing that the actual picture would look less dire?

A lawyer has long been viewed as "an officer of the court" with accompanying obligations of candor. Should an attorney practicing administrative law before an agency be viewed as "an officer of the agency"? Should he have any duty to be sure that the agency is well and fairly informed about the public costs and benefits from a proposed agency action?

Keep in mind that the outcome of the proceeding may affect the costs, health and welfare of many individuals who may be unrepresented (or under-represented) in the case, not just the financial positions of the advocates' clients. Delay and poor regulatory outcomes have real consequences. When lawyers make their presentations or celebrate a regulatory victory, how should they think about those consequences?

EXERCISE 9A — RULEMAKING ETHICS

The factual setting:

The Federal Climate Protection Agency ("FCPA") has promulgated a Notice of Proposed Rulemaking ("NOPR") proposing to address the growing dangers of climate-change impacts from emissions of CO2 and other greenhouse gases. The FCPA's NOPR cites scores of studies demonstrating the near certainty that CO2 and other emissions from burning fossil fuels, especially coal, are contributing to global warming. The studies, which have been done by scientists throughout the world, have led to a broad scientific acceptance that, if not promptly limited, emissions of CO2 and other greenhouse gases are very likely to raise average worldwide temperatures by two to four degrees Celsius, and could raise temperatures by even more, within the next 50–90 years. The studies draw on several lines of research, including into current and historic relationships between greenhouse gases and temperature, chemistry, physics, sources and sinks of greenhouse gases, meteorology, and other fields. (A few recent reports summarizing the science of climate change are included in the **LEXISNEXIS WEBCOURSE**).

The NOPR explains that the likely consequences of human-induced climate change are severe for the health and welfare of people living throughout the world, including in the United States. Probable outcomes include extreme weather, severe agricultural and economic disruption, water shortages, spreading diseases, loss of species, acidification of the oceans with consequential loss of sea life and a human food source, mass migrations, and possible armed conflicts. Since the "half life" of atmospheric CO2 is very long, much of the CO2 emitted today will remain in the atmosphere for centuries. Consequently, it is necessary to start action sooner rather than later. The NOPR also notes that coal emissions in the U.S. contribute to an estimated 15,000 premature deaths and many thousands more cases of illness every year, so reducing coal burning would be beneficial even apart from climate change.

The NOPR proposes limited action at this time: it would require large coal-fired boilers to reduce emissions through co-firing natural gas for 50% of their heat output within five years. Conversion to natural gas would cost money, the agency explains, but there is no question about the technical feasibility of this partial solution. The FCPA explains that there is an abundance of natural gas in the U.S. and burning natural gas will reduce CO2 emissions substantially. The higher fuel costs, its analysis shows, will be more than offset by the long-term savings from mitigating climate change.

Your client is the Association for the Advancement of Mining and Manufacturing. AAMM wants you to file comments on the FCPA rulemaking proposal to limit emissions of greenhouse gases. It wants hard-hitting comments disputing the Notice of Proposed Rulemaking's underlying premise that climate is changing due to human-driven emissions of CO2 and "so-called greenhouse gases."

AAMM's executive director, Wylie Smoke, is a long-time veteran of Washington politics. He knows that, someday, there might be regulation of greenhouse gas emissions, but, in his view, delay is a victory for the trade association and its manufacturing members.

He wants to file comments arguing that the studies claiming anthropogenic global warming are bogus and fraught with uncertainty. As long as there is any uncertainty, he argues, the government should let utilities, manufacturers, and mining companies continue their business without further interference until the science is beyond question. He tells you to talk to AAMM's in-house expert and write devastatingly strong comments. "Raise every possible argument. Our members want us to stop these regulations, and we intend to do just that."

You meet with the in-house expert. He is an engineer who has read lots of studies and critical websites, but he is not a climate scientist. When you speak with him, you hear a litany of criticisms of some of the studies cited by the agency's NOPR. For each of the major studies, he cites an assumption here or an inference there as being debatable.

When you ask whether he's saying that there is no significant danger of human-caused global warming and that all the climate science is simply wrong, he brushes the question aside. "Of course I'm skeptical. They can't predict the weather tomorrow, how can they be sure what will happen in 50 or 100 years."

You ask if he has reviewed the NOPR, which cites scores of studies and meta-studies to conclude that man-made warming is highly probable particularly as a result of CO_2 emissions, and that, if steps are not taken soon to reduce emissions, warming could produce severe harm to people and economies. When you press for the details of his criticisms, you find they are second hand to him, that they are highly technical criticisms which might alter the degree, but not the trend of global warming. He also says that, based on his review of criticisms available on the Internet, he would like the organization to assert that the "science supporting regulation is highly politicized" and that available evidence suggests that the world is just going through a temporary phase. He cannot believe that the future of industrial policies would be based on "paleo-climate" studies or 100-year weather models.

When you ask for his basis, he cites some websites which he finds persuasive. You ask what the relative probability is that the agency is wrong or that the critics are wrong? He says AAMM is confident that, either way, its members will be better off beating back the regulations. He knows some outside consultants who will support their position.

You also ask what the public consequences would be if he and AAMM are wrong and emissions continue to build while some businesses demand certainty? He concedes that CO_2 can persist in the atmosphere for hundreds or even thousands of years after it is emitted, but that's a "down-the-road" problem. "Sure," he says, "if they're right, the problems could be severe in parts of the world and delaying a solution might make things worse. We just don't believe that their confidence level is high enough."

You ask if he has talked to scientists within AAMM's members. "Most don't have their own scientists," he says. "Some do and some of them have written to us acknowledging that global warming is a real problem which should be addressed sooner rather than later. But, we view those member statements as confidential. Anyway, the board of AAMM makes the call, and those guys are in the minority."

Back with the Executive Director, Mr. Smoke repeats that he wants you to file hard-hitting comments emphasizing the uncertainty of the rulemaking's assumptions and conclusions and demanding that the agency abandon its NOPR. "Uncertainty is a winner. We want you to argue that the warming forecasts are expensive guesses," the Executive Director tells you. "Our expert will help you highlight every possible flaw in the global warming science. Say that the proposal is driven by politics. Emphasize uncertainty as to causes, how fast global warming might emerge and what, if any, harm it might do." "Be realistic," he adds. "This is Washington. Our congressional allies need us to attack global warming predictions as being unscientific and filled with uncertainty. If you make those arguments strongly, those guys will take care of us. It won't matter what the agency concludes."

Think about a lawyer's roles and duties and the issues raised by the hypothetical rulemaking and your client's proposed strategy. Also look over the American Bar Association's Rules of Professional Responsibility which can be found online at

http://www.americanbar.org/groups/professional_responsibility/ publications/mod el_rules_of_professional_conduct /model_rules_of_professional_conduct_table_of _contents.html

How helpful are these rules? A number of provisions of the Model Rules are potentially relevant. Which did you identify? Here are some.

The Preamble: A Lawyer's Responsibilities, for example, states: "[1] A lawyer, as a member of the legal profession, is a representative of clients, an officer of the legal system and a public citizen having special responsibility for the quality of justice." It also states "[16] . . . The Rules do not . . . exhaust the moral and ethical considerations that should inform a lawyer, for no worthwhile human activity can be completely defined by legal rules."

Rule 3.9 "Advocate in Nonadjudicative Proceedings" directly addresses nonadjudicative proceedings. It incorporates by reference Rules 3.3(a)–(c), 3.4(a)–(c), and 3.5. The cross-referenced provisions and the accompanying commentary clearly prohibit statements known to be "false" but, beyond that, the obligation of "candor toward the tribunal" is somewhat vague. What about misleading a regulatory agency? Curiously, Rule 3.9 does not cross-reference 3.3(d) which compels a lawyer "in an ex parte proceeding" to "inform the tribunal of all material facts known to the lawyer that will enable the tribunal to make an informed decision, whether or not the facts are adverse." This seems somewhat odd given the greater likelihood of *ex parte* communications in rulemakings than in most judicial settings and given the absence of discovery and other tools for assuring that zealous advocacy does not produce unjust results. On the other hand, the commentary to Rule 3.9 states that a lawyer must deal with the decision-making body "honestly" and "the decision-making body, like a court should be able to rely on the integrity of the submissions to it."

Among the other relevant rules is "Rule 8.4 Misconduct" which states "It is professional misconduct for a lawyer to: (c) engage in conduct involving dishonesty, fraud, deceit or misrepresentation; (d) engage in conduct that is prejudicial to the administration of justice."

These highlight some but not all of the potentially relevant ethical rules. In any event, as noted above, these model rules do not end the inquiry. Other factors, including one's moral sense and views of integrity come into play.

With this background, how would you answer the following questions? (If, as a personal matter, you are a "climate skeptic," accept for the sake of discussion that the objective evidence and scientific consensus supports the conclusions that human emissions of CO_2 and other chemicals are the primary cause of climate change and that there is a very high probability that global warming is causing and will cause serious public harm to health, economies, agriculture, water supplies, oceans, and other species.)

1. Do you have a duty to your client to make the arguments he wants?

2. Do you have a duty to question your client about his factual claims or his claims of uncertainty? Does the fact that your client will not be subject to cross-examination or discovery affect your view on this?

3. (a) Do you have an ethical or moral duty to the agency or the public to temper the arguments your client wants to make if AAMM's proposed uncertainty arguments exaggerate the problems with an objective review of the evidence? (b) Should you disclose that the sources of the criticisms (*e.g.*, interest group websites or that some of AAMM's members have acknowledged both the reality of global warming and the need to act) even if it reveals weaknesses in your client's position? (c) Should your comments put the trade-offs in perspective, for example, by disclosing that even your client's expert concedes that the public harms would be very substantial if the agency's global warming forecasts are correct?

4. Would your answer be changed if the agency's rules were to include the following statement:

Subscription and verification.

(a) Subscription. (1) Any filing with the Commission must be signed.

(2) The signature on a filing constitutes a certificate that:

(i) The signer has read the filing signed and knows its contents;

(ii) The contents are true as stated, to the best knowledge and belief of the signer; and

(iii) The signer possesses full power and authority to sign the filing.

PART THREE

JUDICIAL REVIEW

OVERVIEW

Issuance of an agency decision may not end the legal process. If your client is adversely affected by a rule or order, it may wish to seek judicial review of the agency's decision. Even if it is not a "party" to the agency proceeding (not all agency proceedings even have "parties"), it may be able to seek judicial review. And, even if it does not seek judicial review, it may decide to intervene in a judicial review proceeding to support either the agency or the challenger.

Whether and when courts will review agency action or a failure to act involve potentially complicated constitutional, statutory, and policy issues. Questions involving the availability of judicial review are expressed as matters of jurisdiction, standing, and sovereign immunity. Availability of review also includes questions under the Administrative Procedure Act and specific substantive statutes, such as the extent to which Congress has precluded judicial review or committed the action under question to agency discretion, thus putting it beyond review. Timing of judicial review is identified by reference to the pendency and maturity of agency actions. Timing involves the doctrines of ripeness and exhaustion of administrative remedies. It may also involve the doctrine of primary jurisdiction — whether an action is best initiated in an agency or a court.

Assuming a case has been brought in a timely fashion by a proper litigant in the proper forum, the next set of important judicial review questions go to the applicable standard of judicial review and the scope of that standard. Section 706(2)(E) of the APA, for example, requires that agency findings of fact in formal adjudicatory proceedings be supported by "substantial evidence" in the record. That verbal formulation — "substantial evidence" — constitutes the standard of judicial review to be applied to findings of fact in an adjudicatory case. How that standard is applied, and the likely outcome of the individual cases to which it is applied, gives us some sense of the scope or intensity of the judicial review the standard implies. In short, we are interested not only in determining what standards of judicial review courts will apply in various factual policy and legal contexts, but also in the scope or intensity of judicial review that then results.

This determination inevitably leads to broader issues such as what the purposes of judicial review of agency action should be. We know that administrative agencies are created by Congress to carry out certain statutorily defined duties. One major purpose of judicial review, therefore, is to assure that agencies exercise their powers in accordance with the substantive goals and limits prescribed by Congress. If an agency could freely act in an *ultra vires* manner, its decisions would undercut completely separation-of-powers principles. Article I, Section 706(2)(C) of the APA gives courts the power to set aside agency action found to be "in excess of statutory jurisdiction, authority, or limitations, or short of statutory right."

Similarly, an agency cannot engage in activities which, though authorized by statute, are unconstitutional. This power is reflected in section 706(2) (B) of the APA which authorizes a court to hold unlawful or to set aside agency action found to be "contrary to constitutional right, power, privilege, or immunity."

The need to examine *what* agencies can and cannot do substantively is tied to the separation-of-powers principles. If agencies could interpret their statutes in such a way as to give themselves powers the legislature or the Constitution does not authorize, they would clearly violate separation-of-powers principles, no matter what approach they took to such issues.

The APA, also authorizes courts to examine *how* agencies exercise their substantive powers — that is, the procedures they employ and the justifications they give in reaching their decisions. Without the procedural constraints imposed by the Consti-tution and statutes, an agency might freely act outside its statutory powers or beyond the Constitution itself. More important, the procedures an agency uses when it exercises its substantive powers inevitably involve values that go to the heart of agency legitimacy. These values include fairness, openness, public participation, rational decision-making, and the need for agencies to wield their power in such a way as to make the unelected agency officials involved accountable to the legislative, executive, and judicial branches of government. Thus, section 706(2) (A) of the APA provides that agency rules must not be "arbitrary, capricious or an abuse of discretion," and section 706(2) (D) provides that courts set aside agency action that is "without observance of procedure required by law."

Within the boundaries imposed by statutes and the Constitution, administrative agencies are expected to show judgment, expertise and initiative in carrying out the law. Faithful implementation of the law thus requires agencies to exercise considerable discretion not only in *what* they decide, but in *how* they decide the issues before them. The scope of their discretion, in turn, imposes limits on the scope of judicial review. Judges may not simply substitute their judgments for the reasoned judgments of administrators.

In considering the scope of judicial review of agency findings of fact or interpretations of law or the creation of new agency policies, a number of institutional questions are raised that involve the respective decision-making roles that courts should play. Sorting out these roles and determining the extent to which a court should or should not defer to an agency in various contexts can raise important theoretical as well as statutory and constitutional issues.

Finally, as we assess and attempt to apply basic principles of judicial review of agency action and the legislation on which it is based, we cannot disregard the overall social and political context in which courts operate. This context is usually reflected in the enabling statutes that govern agency action, the makeup and characteristics of the agencies themselves, and the nature of their regulatory tasks. Theory aside, individual judges can also bring their political views to cases reviewing administrative actions. The standards of judicial review are supposed to help constrain judges, as well as agencies.

Judicial Review for the Practitioner

For practicing attorneys, application of these concepts to a given client's objections to an agency's actions is ultimately very practical: how do you initiate judicial review, what can you argue, what are the chances of winning, and what would it mean to win?

Judicial review is not to be lightly undertaken. Although your client may feel it will be harmed by an agency's action, judicial review is expensive and the odds are generally stacked in favor of the agency by deferential standards of review. As a lawyer, you will need to work closely with your client to evaluate whether and how to challenge an unfavorable decision or, in some cases, to defend a favorable one.

As a lawyer, you will need to evaluate a variety of factors when advising your client or implementing your client's desire to seek judicial review.

First, you will need to determine the applicable procedures for seeking judicial review. While the APA will help you fill in blanks, you need to begin with the substantive statute under which the agency acted.

Frequently, the applicable substantive statute or an agency's organizational statute will establish critical elements for judicial review, including timing, jurisdiction, venue, and any special procedures to be employed.

Filing a petition for rehearing at the agency level is sometimes a prerequisite to a petition for judicial review.

If there is no guidance on judicial review in the substantive or organizational statute of a federal agency, your client's only option may be to file a complaint in an appropriate U.S. District Court invoking that court's jurisdiction, under 28 U.S.C. Section § 1331, to decide "Federal questions."

The Federal Rules of Appellate Procedure or the Federal Rules of Civil Procedure, as well as the court's local rules, will need to be consulted for challenges to federal actions.

A challenge to a state agency will generally proceed in state courts, under state law and rules of procedure.

Second, you need to advise your client whether judicial review is available to it. In addition to issues arising under Article III of the Constitution (*e.g.*, standing, justiciability), the agency's substantive statute may further restrict eligibility to challenge an agency's decision.

Are further steps needed to exhaust administrative remedies?

Does your client have standing to seek review?

Are the issues ripe for judicial review?

Has the opportunity for judicial review already passed?

Are the issues your client seeks to raise "justiciable"?

Third, you need to compile and evaluate the legal issues you might raise before a court. For example,

Did the agency adhere — procedurally and substantively — to the words of the applicable statutes, its own regulations, and its prior precedent?

Did it make necessary findings based upon substantial evidence in the record of the proceeding?

Did it reasonably explain its actions, including any departures from its past rulings?

Did it reasonably respond to the issues raised by participants in the proceeding?

Were its actions improperly tainted by violations of "sunshine" laws or any applicable prohibitions against *ex parte* contacts or other improper influences?

What arguments are the agency and other parties likely to raise?

Are there any constitutional questions which can appropriately be raised?

Fourth, you need to realistically advise your client concerning the likelihood of success on the merits.

What are the applicable standards for judicial review and how deferential is a court likely to be to the agency's decision?

How have the courts (particularly the ones you may choose for the appeal) addressed similar issues? When there are venue options, will the choice of the court potentially affect the outcome?

Have you adequately preserved your potential issues and developed a record that will support your arguments?

What counter arguments will you face? Can you persuasively rebut them?

Can you survive a request for dismissal due to possible questions of standing, mootness, ripeness, compliance with applicable procedural rules, etc.?

Fifth, assuming you can persuade the court of the legitimacy of your client's position, what remedies could you request and what remedies are you likely to obtain from the court? In other words, what will it mean to "win"?

Is it realistic to think the court might vacate the order below or reverse and remand with directions to change a result?

Is it likely to remand for further proceedings to repair a procedural gap or flaw in an explanation, and, if so, are you likely to achieve a different substantive result following a remand?

Does your client need a stay or expedited review of the agency's action to prevent irreparable harm from occurring during the pendency of the appeal? If so, what procedures would you need to follow to request such relief and what are your chances of getting such relief?

In sum, will the plausible outcomes meet the needs of your client?

Sixth, judicial review is expensive and principles of deference stack the odds against the petitioner. You and your client need to consider the costs of seeking or not seeking judicial review and what the alternatives to judicial review might be. For example:

Will the costs of living with the agency ruling be high and can they be mitigated? When confronted with the reality of a final agency decision, clients often decide that they will live with the result and, perhaps upon further reflection, compliance may not be as onerous as they previously argued.

Are there credible strategies for getting relief other than through judicial review (*e.g.*, a petition to the agency for a waiver from, or exception to, a rule; a petition for rehearing or a new rulemaking to address a matter not already considered by the agency; legislation amending the law applied by the agency; executive intervention (*e.g.*, by the Office of Management and Budget); or a long-term lobbying and educational process to try to turn the agency around)?

Would failure to seek judicial review when an order is issued foreclose future challenges to regulations or rulings?

Unless you have a price-insensitive client, your client will want a good estimate of the costs of pursuing judicial review. While it may not be hard to estimate out of pocket costs (*e.g.*, for the filing fee), it is difficult to estimate the hours you and your colleagues are likely to spend writing pleadings (briefs, motions, answers, corporate disclosure documents, etc.), compiling a joint appendix, and preparing for oral argument. Working with an experienced appellate or civil litigator will help you estimate the costs, but even experienced lawyers are often surprised at how many hours a case will require given unforeseen contingencies (*e.g.*, unexpected motions), the desire to polish briefs, and the instinct to pursue exhaustive research.

The ensuing exercises will have you explore the requirements for initiating judicial review of an agency action, and how to pursue the issues.

Webcourse

As background for the exercises, you will find important materials on the **LEXISNEXIS WEBCOURSE**.

In the general materials, you will find excerpts from the Administrative Procedure Act.

In the Appendix and materials for Part One, you will find excerpts from the Natural Gas Act, the substantive statute controlling FERC's decision.

In the materials for Part Three, you will find parts of the Federal Rules of Appellate Procedure and the D.C. Circuit's local rules and handbook. (If your case is in a different court, you will need to locate the applicable rules for that court.)

For the sake of illustration, we have also included in the materials for Part Three, excerpts from the records of four judicial review proceedings (district court and appellate), including the docket sheets and selected pleadings. These are included as *examples* of how cases may proceed, not as models to be followed slavishly. (Looking at the docket sheets, you can guess why only excerpts from the records are included.) If you want to see more, the U.S. Courts have an online information system called PACER, which you can investigate.

For particular exercises, there may be references to additional **LEXISNEXIS WEBCOURSE** materials pertaining to specific cases.

Chapter 10

JUDICIAL REVIEW — GETTING STARTED

ESTIMATED TIME FOR COMPLETION: 90 minutes

ESTIMATED LEVEL OF DIFFICULTY: Moderate

In this chapter, you will determine how to initiate a judicial review proceeding in two settings — one from FERC's decision involving North Central Gas Pipeline, Homersville, etc. (Chapters 1–5), and one from the Methyloxystuff rulemaking proceeding (Chapter 8).

These are typical assignments for an administrative lawyer, and it is important to get a sense for the mechanics of initiating review.

EXERCISE 10A — INITIATING JUDICIAL REVIEW OF FERC ACTION

Assume for the purposes of this problem that you represent Homersville (from Part 1). FERC has not yet issued a decision. However, Homersville has asked you to outline the steps that will be needed to initiate a judicial review proceeding if FERC approves North Central's application for a certificate of public convenience and necessity to serve Fantastic. Look at Section 19 of the Natural Gas Act, the Administrative Procedure Act, the applicable federal rules of judicial procedure, and the local rules for the U.S. Court of Appeals for the District of Columbia Circuit, each of which is on the **LEXISNEXIS WEBCOURSE**.

Outline your answers to the following questions for Homersville:

1. What steps, if any, will Homersville need to take before filing for judicial review?

2. Where can it seek judicial review? (Court and venue)?

3. What are the time limits on seeking judicial review?

4. How will it initiate review?

5. Who must it serve?

6. What steps are needed to submit the record or relevant portions of the record to the court?

7. What will be the order of briefing?

8. What if a stay of the agency's action is needed?

EXERCISE 10B — INITIATING JUDICIAL REVIEW OF FEA ACTION

Assume your firm represents an entity that filed comments in the Chapter 8 rulemaking concerning Methyloxystuff. Before an order is issued, a partner in your firm wants to know what the firm's client will need to do to challenge the agency's action if the final rule is unfavorable. Since you are the first associate the partner can find at 5:30 p.m. on a Friday evening, she asks you to figure out the answer. She says she doesn't need a full memo yet, but she wants a brief outline of the answers for her before she has a phone call with the client on Monday.

You review the statute empowering the FEA to regulate emissions of toxic substances, such as Methyloxystuff, and find nothing about judicial review. Likewise, the FEA's organizational statute is silent. With that in mind, answer the following questions:

1. After the agency's final rule is issued, what steps will be needed to obtain judicial review?

2. Will your client need to take any particular steps at the agency before filing for judicial review?

3. Where can it seek judicial review?

4. What might be done to expedite the case?

EXERCISE 10C — STANDING

Assume you are an attorney in the FERC Solicitor's office. You have received petitions for judicial review from all of the parties that filed protests in the North Central Gas Pipeline certificate docket. Each of those petitioners describes its standing to the court in approximately the same terms as it described its interest before the FERC. Each filed or joined in a petition for rehearing. In the docketing statements for their appeals to the D.C. Circuit, the petitioners set forth the basis for their standing as follows:

Town of Homersville:

"Homersville, MN operates a municipal natural gas utility which serves residents and businesses located within the Town, and immediate surrounding areas. Homersville has been a firm natural gas transportation customer of North Central for over 20 years, and all of Homersville's natural gas supplies are transported by North Central.

"Homersville is adversely affected by FERC's orders granting North Central's certificate application in at least three respects. *First*, North Central's direct deliveries to Fantastic Manufacturing will bypass Homersville's gas utility services and deprive Homersville of its largest customer. Fantastic uses more natural gas than all of Homersville's other customers combined. Loss of Fantastic will have severe economic impacts on Homersville and its remaining customers, forcing Homersville to raise rates or taxes to cover the revenue shortfall. *Second*, North Central construction will go through the center of the Homersville Bird Sanctuary, a 500-acre public park and nature preserve, owned and managed by the Town of Homersville. The sanctuary is a major attraction for Homersville's citizens and for tourists who are drawn to the area. Construction through the bird sanctuary will cause extensive, permanent damage and limit the public's future use and enjoyment of the sanctuary. Pipeline construction through the park will harm an endangered species that has been seen in the sanctuary. *Third*, FERC's order failed to relieve Homersville of an unjust and unreasonable contract extension, which North Central unfairly obtained from Homersville just before North Central announced its agreement to serve Fantastic, thereby eliminating Homersville's need for half the volumes of the extended contract."

Homersville Audubon Society:

"The Homersville Audubon Society is an association of bird watchers and nature enthusiasts who live in or near Homersville, MN. HAS has a membership of approximately 80 individuals. Members of HAS regularly utilize the Homersville Bird Sanctuary (Sanctuary) for bird watching and nature walks. Some members of HAS volunteer to lead small groups to observe birds, animals, flowers and trees located in the Sanctuary. Most members of HAS are residents of Homersville whose taxes help support the Sanctuary. Some members make charitable donations to help support the Sanctuary.

"This case involves review of North Central's certificate application to construct and operate pipeline facilities running through the Homersville Bird Sanctuary, a major attraction for HAS members as well other residents in the Homersville area. FERC's orders granting North Central a certificate of public convenience and necessity will permanently damage the Sanctuary and harm an endangered species of bird found in the Sanctuary. HAS and its members are aggrieved by FERC's orders and the resulting degradation of the Sanctuary and the habitat and species within it."

Homersville Taxpayers Alliance:

"The Homersville Taxpayers Alliance is an unincorporated association of eleven citizens who live and pay taxes in Homersville, MN. Members of HTA live in Homersville and pay taxes to support Homersville. HTA was formed to oppose taxes and wasteful spending by Homersville. Two HTA members utilize the Homersville Bird Sanctuary (Sanctuary) for nature walks.

"This case involves review of FERC orders approving a certificate application to construct and operate pipeline facilities running through the Homersville Bird Sanctuary. The Sanctuary is owned and managed by the Town of Homersville and therefore has been paid for by the citizens of Homersville, including HTA members. As a result of FERC's orders, the Sanctuary will be subject to damaging construction and to a taking by eminent domain. Taxpayer dollars spent to make the bird sanctuary the best in the region will have been wasted, and HTA members' enjoyment of the Sanctuary will be hurt. The loss of Homersville's largest customer will presumably cause Homersville to raise natural gas rates or taxes to make up for the lost revenues. Consequently, HTA and its members are aggrieved by the FERC orders being reviewed and by this latest instance of Federal interference in local affairs."

International Birders Union:

"The IBU is an international association of bird watchers which includes a number of U.S. residents. IBU's members visit parks, refuges and other locations in the U.S. and around the world in search of rare birds. The IBU's statement of organizational purpose strongly supports the formation and preservation of bird sanctuaries.

"IBU has standing to obtain judicial review of FERC's orders approving North Central's pipeline project. Although IBU is not aware that any member has yet visited the Homersville Bird Sanctuary, it is aware from informational exchanges on its "bird hotline" that some members have visited other sanctuaries in search of the remaining examples of William's Flycatcher. Since William's Flycatcher is a migratory species, harm to it in any part of its range will reduce the chances that IBU's members will spot the species in other parts of its range. Also, because its members travel far and wide to spot rare birds, IBU is confident that some of its members will visit the Homersville Bird Sanctuary in the future if the sanctuary is not damaged by the construction of North Central's proposed pipeline."

Mid-Central Pipeline Company:

"Mid-Central Pipeline Company operates an interstate pipeline extending across seven States. Mid-Central's mainline passes roughly eight miles from the Homersville plant site of Fantastic Manufacturing Company. Mid-Central offers open-access transportation and stands ready, willing and able to provide firm and interruptible transportation service to Fantastic.

"This case involves review of North Central's certificate application to construct and operate pipeline facilities running through the Homersville Bird Sanctuary. The Homersville Bird Sanctuary is a valuable environmental resource, which is well-known in Minnesota and surrounding States. Granting a certificate of public convenience and necessity to North Central would harm the Bird Sanctuary and its many assets, including the wildlife that live in it.

"Mid-Central is capable of building a pipeline that would serve Fantastic's needs using existing rights of way and avoiding any construction in the Homersville Bird Sanctuary. Although Mid-Central would require somewhat more construction to reach Fantastic's plant, the additional cost (approximately $2.1 million) would be money well spent in order to minimize environmental harm from pipeline construction. By failing to prepare an environmental impact statement or conduct a comparative hearing, FERC failed to fairly consider the pro-environmental alternative offered by Mid-Central."

Minnesota Audubon League:

In addition to the parties to the proceeding below, the Minnesota Audubon League filed a timely petition for judicial review of the FERC's decision and joined the petition for rehearing filed by the Homersville Audubon Society (HAS) even though it did not move to intervene in the FERC proceeding. It made the following statement concerning standing:

"The Minnesota Audubon League is the largest environmental and bird-watcher organization in the State of Minnesota. Since HAS is a chapter of the Minnesota Audubon League, the League treats HAS's members as automatically being members of the League. As a result, League members use and value the Homersville Bird Sanctuary. Harm to the Sanctuary will result from North Central's FERC-authorized construction. As a result, the League and its members are harmed by the FERC orders under review, and the League has standing to vindicate its interests and the interests of its members."

Your boss, the FERC Solicitor, asks you which of these petitioners really has Article III standing, and which petitions for review might be dismissed by the court of appeals. He notes that, just because FERC allowed a party to intervene in the agency's case, does not mean they would survive scrutiny by the court. FERC rarely makes a judgment about standing at the agency level although it could certainly do so. Its normal practice is to automatically grant unopposed motions to intervene. It is easier to let parties into a case and address their issues than to risk excluding a party who actually has standing.

With that instruction from the agency's Solicitor, look at the information above and, for each petitioner, advise the Solicitor whether a motion to dismiss on grounds of standing is worth pursuing. Just to remind you, the petitioners for judicial review from the FERC's decision are:

Town of Homersville

Homersville Audubon Society

Homersville Taxpayers Alliance

International Birders Union

Mid-Central Pipeline Company

Minnesota Audubon League

Chapter 11

THE APPELLATE CHALLENGE

ESTIMATED TIME FOR COMPLETION: 90 minutes

ESTIMATED LEVEL OF DIFFICULTY: Difficult

Unfortunately, the agency approved North Central's certificate application as filed and rejected the protests and hearing requests by Homersville and its allies, as well as their rehearing requests and motions for stay. The agency ruled based solely on the pleadings without conducting further proceedings. It summarily rejected the rehearing requests.

After listening to your summary of the decision, Bob Marshall of Homersville tells you that the Town Council is so upset about the impact of the decision that it wants judicial review of FERC's orders and the legal fees will not be a barrier to an appeal.

He then directs you to prepare a petition for judicial review in the U.S. Court of Appeals for the District of Columbia Circuit and proceed with drafting the brief and figuring out how to stop the construction.

For purposes of doing the exercises, your professor will release to you, with the **LEXISNEXIS WEBCOURSE**, the key elements of the agency record, including the agency decisions and the pleadings.

We suggest that you do Exercise 11A and choose either Exercise 11B or 11C.

EXERCISE 11A — DRAFTING A PETITION FOR REVIEW

Draft Homersville's petition for judicial review, which you have decided to file in the U.S. Court of Appeals for the District of Columbia Circuit. (A sample of a petition for review is available on the **LEXISNEXIS WEBCOURSE** as part of the record for *Apache v. FERC*.)

EXERCISE 11B — DRAFTING PARTS OF THE PETITIONER'S BRIEF

Based on the webcourse materials (record, regulations, law) and your knowledge of administrative law, write the following portions of your initial brief for the petitioner:

(a)   The Statement of Issues

(b)   The Summary of Argument (not more than 5 pages).

EXERCISE 11C — DRAFTING A MOTION FOR STAY OF FERC'S ORDER

Obviously, the appeal will do little good for the bird sanctuary and William's Flycatcher if the pipeline right-of-way is cleared before the court decides the case.

In order to obtain a stay, you will need to file a motion that persuades the court that a stay is justified under a four-part standard spelled out in *Virginia Petroleum Jobbers Association v. FPC, 104 U.S. App. D.C. 106, 259 F.2d 921 (1958)*:

(1)   Has the petitioner made a strong showing that it is likely to prevail on the merits of its appeal?

(2)   Has the petitioner shown that without such relief, it will be irreparably injured?

(3)   Would the issuance of a stay substantially harm other parties interested in the proceedings?

(4)   Where lies the public interest?

Note that the D.C. Circuit has held that satisfying the first prong — probability of success on the merits — does not necessarily require a demonstration that overturning the agency is more probable than not. Instead, the court will consider a lesser showing on the likelihood of success if the showings on the other three issues weigh heavily in favor of the party requesting a stay. *Washington Metropolitan Area Transit Commission v. Holiday Tours, Inc.*, 559 F.2d 841 *(D.C.Cir. 1977)*. If there is a question about the court's jurisdiction or the petitioner's standing, such issues will also be considered in connection with the first prong.

Your tasks:

•   With that background, would you advise your client to file a motion for a stay?

•   Regardless of how you answered that question, draft a motion for stay (or at least the portion addressing the four factors) to the U.S. Court of Appeals for the District of Columbia Circuit, which is the court of appeals your client has chosen based on the options permitted by Section 19 of the Natural Gas Act. Note that the D.C. Circuit Handbook, as well as the Federal Rules of Appellate Procedure and the D.C. Circuit's local rules, are on the **LEXISNEXIS WEBCOURSE**. The Handbook notes, among other things, that a motion for stay is deemed a procedural motion which is to be filed within 30 days. Examples of motions for stays are also included in the **LEXISNEXIS WEBCOURSE** for Part 3.

Chapter 12

JUDICIAL REVIEW AND ENFORCEMENT ACTIONS

ESTIMATED TIME FOR COMPLETION: 60 minutes

ESTIMATED LEVEL OF DIFFICULTY: Difficult

The timing of judicial review is important. An attempt to seek review may be too early or may be too late. You may need to develop a strategy for creating a reviewable decision. This chapter invites you to consider the availability of judicial review for a rule that is already on the books.

EXERCISE 12A — CHALLENGING AN EXISTING RULE

The "Federal Emissions Agency" issued a rule in 2007 prescribing certain limitations on particulates and other emissions by cement manufacturers. According to the rule, all cement manufacturers were required to install equipment to limit emissions of various forms of air pollution by shutting down or installing air pollution control equipment within three years. The relevant statute governing pollution from cement manufacturers states that an appellate challenge to a rule or order issued by the FEA must be filed in the U.S. Court of Appeals for the District of Columbia Circuit within 60 days after a rule is issued. No petitions for review of the 2007 rule were filed.

Your client, Housing Cement, Inc., is a new company that manufactures cement. It didn't exist in 2007, but was created in 2010 when your client acquired a 20-year old company, which had not taken any steps to comply with the 2007 rule. The law firm that was supposed to do the regulatory due diligence for the acquisition failed to catch the fact that the acquisition target faced a compliance deadline that it clearly was not going to meet.

Your client has now been assessed a fine for violating the 2007 rule by failing to install any pollution control equipment. After reviewing the 2007 rule and rule making record, you conclude that the order assessing the penalty is invalid because the 2007 rule exceeded the agency's statutory authority and because the rule wasn't based on reasoned consideration of the record. Specifically, you question the FEA's authority to issue the rule in its current form because the relevant statute excludes "home building materials" and "manufacturers of home building materials" from the emissions rules that the FEA may issue. In the rule making, FEA held that manufacturers of cement are not exempt as "manufacturers of home building materials" because the FEA's data show that the majority of cement produced in the U.S. is used for constructing roads, commercial buildings and industrial uses, not for new dwelling units.

You note that the statute does not have a "majority-use" standard; it simply exempts "manufacturers of home building materials." Your client estimates that, in most years, more than half of the cement it manufactures winds up in new homes and apartment buildings. You want to argue that the exemption should be applied on the basis of the manufacturing and sales patterns of individual manufacturers, not that the cement industry should be exempt based on average statistics. The House-Senate Conference Report for the statute highlighted the virtues of home building and the need to protect home building from burdensome costs, but it did not otherwise address the exemption question.

Prepare a memo to your client outlining your recommended strategy for challenging the penalty, the expected response from the agency, and the likelihood of success of your various arguments.

EXERCISE 12B — RIPENESS

Assume that the agency has not assessed a penalty. Instead, one of its inspectors has written a letter to your client informing your client that it will have to achieve full compliance within 12 months or face a large fine.

Would you recommend a different strategy? Is such a letter from an inspector a sufficiently final action to support judicial review?

Chapter 13

JUDICIAL REVIEW OF A RULE

ESTIMATED TIME FOR COMPLETEION: 90 minutes

ESTIMATED LEVEL OF DIFFICULTY: Difficult

A central issue in judicial review of actions by administrative agencies is the extent to which the courts are expected to defer to the agency's findings and conclusions of fact and law. Depending on the underlying statute and the type of issue, deference may or may not be required. Many court decisions are devoted to the deference issue and much ink has been spilled by commentators over this issue. While most attention has been paid to the federal case law, it is important to recognize that, if you are in a state judicial review proceeding, the analysis may be different.

The issue, of course, is not merely academic. The outcome of any given case may turn on the extent to which judges defer to the decisions issued by administrative agencies.

The following problem lets you consider these issues, but more than deference lurks in the exercise below.

FACTUAL BACKGROUND FOR EXERCISES 13A-13B

In Chapter 8, you encountered the Federal Emissions Agency (FEA) rulemaking concerning "methyloxystuff" and "best available control technology" ("BACT"). That rulemaking was initiated ten months before the end of a Democratic Administration. However, it was not concluded before a new Republican Administration took office. When the agency finally acted, a new Administrator was in place. Having come from a conservative think tank, he had very different views from his predecessor about environmental issues.

The final rule was issued four months after the new Administrator was appointed. In the preamble to the final rule, the FEA declares that Methyloxystuff is, in fact, a hazardous pollutant. The agency finds that "Methyloxystuff" can cause asthma, emphysema, and cancer. Children within 15 miles of a source are particularly vulnerable to asthma, and long-term exposure can cause emphysema and several forms of cancer (lung and colon particularly). Beyond 30 miles, the incidence of illness drops, but out to 50 miles it is still significantly above the baseline of morbidity found in areas lacking exposure to Methyloxystuff. In great detail, the agency's preamble explains why the studies submitted by the chemical trade associations were flawed. It also explains why steps are needed to limit emissions of Methyloxystuff.

The final rule confirms that "large emitters" of Methyloxystuff will have to install "best available control technology" within two years after the rule is published in the Federal Register. Accepting the comments by Chemicals Galore, the agency's final rule redefines "large emitters" to mean "entities that emit ten tons of Methyloxystuff in any calendar year." The final rule also proceeds to redefine the meaning of "best available control technology."

This BACT requirement is in the applicable statute, the Hazardous Air Pollution Act, which sets forth congressional findings that the statute is needed to afford the public protection from adverse health impacts from chemical pollutants. The statute requires that the Administrator establish standards that mandate implementation of the best available control technology.

> Such standards shall require implementation of the best available control technologies or operating measures or some combination of technologies and techniques designed to reduce hazardous air pollutants to levels that satisfy the air quality criteria established by the Administrator as expeditiously as reasonably practicable.

The BACT standard is more fully spelled out in the agency's regulations. The FEA's general emissions regulations define "best available control technology" as follows:

> Best available control technology" ("BACT") means the best technology available to reduce and minimize hazardous emissions from a stationary source. A technology is considered to be available if it is available commercially or if it has been tested and is reasonably capable of being scaled up to a capacity needed to minimize hazardous emissions from a given source.

For many years, this BACT definition has been interpreted by the FEA to mean that a company would have to install and operate technology which minimizes total emissions from the stationary source, even when the compliance costs to polluters were high and particular technologies were new. This interpretation by FEA has been upheld by the courts against industry challenges.

In the preamble to the Methyloxystuff rule, however, the agency reinterprets "best available control technology" in a manner favorable to emission sources. In explaining the final rule, the agency declares that, going forward, the term "best available control technology" will be interpreted to mean "the most cost-effective means of reducing emissions to a level where such emissions are no longer unreasonably hazardous to exposed populations." As explained in the preamble, rather than requiring companies to install expensive technology to capture hazardous emissions at the source, FEA's new interpretation will permit companies to "do the job of protecting the general population" at lower costs. For example, a company can install very tall smoke stacks or a combination of tall stacks and lower cost (but less effective) emission-reduction equipment, provided that they present a study showing that the pollutant, in this case Methyloxystuff, will be satisfactorily dispersed to acceptable emission concentrations assuming average wind speeds prevailing in the area.

To support its new interpretation, the agency says one should look again at the "words of the statute and its regulations." Since "cheaper is commonly recognized to be better," lower cost technologies should be viewed as the "best" technologies whenever they do "a reasonable job of protecting the general public, not necessarily every subgroup with unique health sensitivities, like asthma." "Trying to protect every possible subgroup," the order explains, "would be unduly costly to jobs and the economy." The agency's preamble declares generally that this interpretation of the applicable statute and its existing regulations is based upon the agency's "expertise," its "many years of experience regulating emissions," and its desire to better balance the costs and benefits of reducing harmful impacts from emissions of Methyloxystuff. Individuals who have special health concerns always have the option to exercise caution, for example, by installing air purifiers, staying indoors, or moving, the preamble notes.

EXERCISE 13A — APPELLATE ISSUES AND ARGUMENTS

You are representing the Save the Lungs Foundation ("SLF"), which has strenuously opposed emissions of Methyloxystuff. Your group has documented the harm that exposure to the chemical can do to children and adults with lung conditions. In your written comments and oral presentation, you presented strong evidence of the adverse health effects, resulting from exposure over time. "Average" daily exposure is obviously important, but harm is caused based on cumulative exposure over time and by shorter, intensive periods of exposure. SLF's research reports, which were included with its comments, indicate that even healthy people may develop lung conditions as a result of Methyloxystuff, though industry-sponsored studies downplay this risk.

Your client is incensed by the outcome of the rulemaking, in particular by the fact that the definition of BACT was even addressed. The notice of proposed rulemaking proposed applying the BACT standard to Methyloxystuff, but the NOPR made no mention of the possibility that this proceeding would be used as a vehicle for reinterpreting a statutory term as basic as "best available control technology." In their comments, a trade association and several manufacturers asked the agency to reduce the compliance burdens faced by emitters of Methyloxystuff, but they did not ask for a wholesale re-write of the "best available control technology" standards.

As to the period of emissions used for identifying a "large emission source," SLF had argued for a much tighter standard: not more than one ton in any month. In the rule making, it presented evidence, including independent health studies and clinical data, showing that very high short-term concentrations of Methyloxystuff are as harmful as long-term emissions. The shift to a calendar-year measure, SLF's general counsel tells you, would increase the potential for highly concentrated emissions over one- to three-month periods. That was the reason Chemicals Galore wanted the calendar-year measure. The agency's final rule accepted Chemical Galore's arguments about regulatory flexibility and its ability to minimize costs, without directly addressing the issue of harm from short-term concentrations.

The Save the Lungs Foundation wants judicial review of the agency's rulings, including its interpretation of its "best available control technology" standard and its relaxation of the emission standard to reflect average emissions and a calendar year standard.

Outline (1) the statement of issues you would recommend that SLF raise, (2) the arguments you would make for why the court should overturn the action, including the level of deference the court should give to the agency's order.

EXERCISE 13B — ARGUING FOR DEFERENCE

As an attorney in the agency's solicitor's office, outline the arguments you would make to the court for the court to pay a high degree of deference to the agency's order.

PART FOUR

INFORMATION AND OPEN GOVERNMENT

OVERVIEW

Information flows to and from the government. It flows to the government in the form of reports, often required by statute, as well as information gleaned from investigations, physical inspections or subpoenas. A great deal of information is provided to the government voluntarily in the form of tax returns or various applications for licenses or permits.

The government also provides information to the public. Today, a great deal of information about federal and state departments and agencies can be found on their websites. Website postings include information about an agency's organization, its programs, regulations, pending cases, rules of procedure, applicable statutes, current and proposed budgets, how to apply for authorizations or grants, and how to apply for information under applicable statutes. Some of the posted information is educational, including for example, reports to Congress, historical or cultural information, industry data, "how to . . ." instructions (*e.g.*, how to apply for grants or save energy or plant corn or test soil), "where to find . . ." guidance, etc. Some organizations, such as the Congressional Budget Office or the General Accounting Office publish in-depth reports on various aspects of government programs, including costs, assessments of effectiveness, and criticisms. The Congress and the Library of Congress may also have useful information. Particularly when you are new to an area of administrative practice, do not hesitate to review the websites of the relevant agencies to get a sense of what those agencies do, how they do it, and how you can approach the agencies to provide input or get information on behalf of your client.

One of the most significant developments in the area of public information is the advent of statutes requiring the federal government and agencies in many state governments to provide information in response to specific written requests submitted by members of the public. In the late 1960s and throughout the 1970s, Congress passed a number of statutes aimed at increasing the openness with which federal agencies carried out their regulatory responsibilities. Foremost among these was the Freedom of Information Act (FOIA), first passed in 1966. It and its subsequent amendments establish a liberal disclosure policy regarding public access to information obtained, generated, and held by the government. "Any person" is entitled to request and receive identifiable records held by an agency, unless the records in question fall within one of the Act's nine exemptions. The burden of denying disclosure is on the government.

Freedom of information laws have proved extremely useful for the media, advocacy groups, and citizens. In some cases, it may have been used in ways not initially anticipated. For example, it can be an important discovery tool in litigation with agencies, quite apart from the more general goals of providing the information our democracy needs to function well. Information requests, particularly for complete email histories, have become a tool for advocacy groups which seek to find provocative email chatter that might embarrass scientists and others whose research conflicts with the advocates' political or economic goals.

Moreover, as FOIA has become so important in a variety of contexts, the volume of requests agencies receive has grown exponentially. The expense agencies incur in responding to these requests creates a number of problems including, of course, delay in agency responses, raising issues of enforcement.

The importance of FOIA is evidenced, in part, by the availability of FOIA guidelines on every federal agency's website and by a lengthy report on FOIA requirements published by the Department of Justice. It is available online at http://www.justice.gov/oip/foia_guide09.htm. The Internet also has privately run websites devoted to educating the public on how to use FOIA at the federal and state levels. One example is a website run by the Reporters Committee for Freedom of the Press, which addresses freedom of information and sunshine laws: http://www.rcfp.org/federal-open-government-guide/introduction and http://www.rcfp.org/open-government-guide.

In 1972, Congress passed the Federal Advisory Committee Act (FACA) designed to ensure greater openness with regard to the various boards of experts and advisors that agencies sometimes rely upon for advice. FACA was the forerunner of the Government in the Sunshine Act passed in 1976 and intended to establish a norm of openness for agency deliberations. The Act thus requires that most meetings of multimember commissions be noticed in advance and held in public. Congress also passed the Federal Privacy Act in 1974. Unlike the Acts described above, this Act deals with individuals. The premise of the Act is that the federal government's ability to use sophisticated information technology, such as computer data banks, greatly magnifies the potential for the harm that can result to individual privacy interests. The assumption underlying all of this legislation is that open government leads to better government. Open government is in accord with our basic principles of democracy and the need for citizens to know how their government, in fact, functions.

Nearly all States have some form of open government laws. Provisions include requirements allowing public access to meetings and to documents. Not surprisingly, state laws and policies vary substantially.

The exercises that follow will address some of these issues. The **LEXISNEXIS WEBCOURSE** includes several documents relevant to information and open government. These include the federal FOIA, Privacy Act, and Sunshine Act, and guidance from the White House and Attorney General concerning FOIA compliance. There is a citizen handbook for FOIA published by Congress. There is also a compilation of illustrative materials concerning Virginia's sunshine laws.

Chapter 14

PREPARING A FOIA REQUEST

ESTIMATED TIME FOR COMPLETION: 60 minutes

ESTIMATED LEVEL OF DIFFICULTY: Moderate

When you met with Bob Marshall, back in Part One, he told you that, according to Fantastic's vice president, Tom Clark, representatives of North Central and Homersville had met with senior members of the Federal Energy Regulatory Commission staff two weeks before the pipeline filed its certificate application at FERC. Mr. Clark said that their meeting had gone well. He said that they told the staff how much the bypass would cost to build, how much Fantastic hoped to save each year, and how much those savings would mean to the economics of Fantastic's plant in Homersville, including a possible future expansion. He said the staff had made some suggestions about what to say in the application.

Mr. Marshall said that he asked Mr. Clark if they had informed the FERC staff about the potential harms to Homersville and its customers or the bird sanctuary. He said they had not. When the staff representatives had asked if there would be opposition, North Central's lawyer said they thought it was possible. Mr. Clark said he could not remember their names, but North Central had said they were senior advisors to the Commission on gas pipeline projects, including a lawyer and someone from the environmental group. Mr. Clark thought that one of the staffers may have been the Director of Pipeline Regulation.

Mr. Clark added that the North Central lawyer used to work for FERC, and he obviously had close relations with the FERC representatives with whom they met. After the meeting, North Central's lawyer reportedly said that getting approval of the certificate to do the bypass shouldn't be a problem. Sensing Mr. Marshall's annoyance, Mr. Clark got defensive and would not disclose anything else about the meeting.

Mr. Marshall wants to know what you can find out about the meeting between the staff, North Central, and Fantastic. In particular, Mr. Marshall wants to know who attended and what was said at the meeting by representatives of North Central,

Fantastic, and the FERC staff representatives. He also would like copies of any documents that were given to the staff and any notes or memos prepared by the staff either for their own files or for their superiors. If there are records of other discussions with the staff, he would like to know about them.

Preparing a FOIA request is not difficult *per se*. FOIA requests may be submitted by any person, not just a lawyer. Only a letter is required, not a formal pleading.

Getting timely answers, however, may be difficult, particularly if the request requires reviews of large files or production of many documents or if it the request targets documents that address exempt topics, like certain internal deliberations. Also, you need to recognize that fees may be associated with copying materials. Consequently, writing an effective FOIA request takes some thought. In the interest of expedition and cost, it may be desirable to focus the request as precisely as you can (time period, particular offices or individuals' files, subject matter, etc.).

EXERCISE 14A — FOIA BASICS

Go to the FERC website (www.ferc.gov) and under "Legal Resources" look at FERC's procedure for receiving and processing FOIA requests. (FERC's FOIA regulations can be found at 18 C.F.R Part 388 Information and Requests.) FERC offers a choice of submitting a request electronically or in writing. Start by answering the following basic questions:

Assuming you choose to submit in writing, to whom should the request be addressed?

What needs to be included in the letter?

If you submit a request to collect information on North Central's pre-filing meeting with the FERC staff five weeks before Homersville's protest is due, can you expect to get the information before an intervention and protest is due to be filed? If not, can you expedite processing of the request?

EXERCISE 14B — DRAFT A FOIA REQUEST

Prepare a FOIA request (or FOIA requests) asking for the information you would like concerning North Central's and Fantastic's contacts with the FERC staff. Try to be as specific as possible in order to increase the chances you can get the information in a timely manner.

What objections do you anticipate you may receive and would they be valid? Specifically, might any of the nine exemptions to FOIA disclosure apply to any part of the request you are making?

Chapter 15

FOIA AND PRIVATE ENTITIES

ESTIMATED TIME FOR COMPLETION: 60 minutes

ESTIMATED LEVEL OF DIFFICULTY: Moderate

FOIA requests must be addressed to a government agency. To the extent the government agency has documents with confidential personal or corporate information in its files, private parties may have grounds to object to release of that information. Other issues are raised if the government has a private entity perform governmental functions on its behalf.

In reviewing Appendix I to the FERC's blanket certificate regulations for certain transactions, including construction of minor facilities (18 C.F.R. Part 157, Subpart F), you notice the following statement:

> [T]he certificate holder shall, upon acceptance of its blanket certificate, be designated as the Commission's non-federal representative to the U.S. Fish and Wildlife Services (FWS) . . . in order to conduct informal consultations with those agencies.

In effect, FERC delegates to the pipeline the duty to consult with FWS in connection with the Endangered Species Act. You recall that, in its application, North Central claims to have obtained FWS' concurrence that there were no endangered or threatened species or critical habitat which would be affected by the proposed construction.

Since you have been told by Mr. Marshall, the Homersville Audubon Society and a professor of biology that William's Flycatcher has been spotted multiple times in the area, you want to know exactly what communications occurred between North Central and USFWS and what North Central may have known that it did not convey to USFWS or FERC. You are also interested in communications between FERC and USFWS.

The FOIA, of course, only goes to government records. But, you reason, North Central was acting as FERC's representative. Does that give you an opportunity to extend the FOIA request to North Central directly or indirectly through FERC?

EXERCISE 15 — FOIA STRATEGY

Outline a FOIA strategy for seeking documents that North Central exchanged with USFWS or FERC and any documents North Central may have in its files which would be relevant to the endangered species issue. What arguments could be made for and against you receiving the information? Rate your chances of getting any such documents.

Would there be any benefits from asking for the records even if you do not get them?

What about using FOIA to get information about FERC-USFWS communications related to North Central's application?

Chapter 16

SUNSHINE LAWS AND OPEN MEETING REQUIREMENTS

ESTIMATED TIME FOR COMPLETION: 60 minutes

ESTIMATED LEVEL OF DIFFICULTY: Moderate

The federal government and most states have statutes requiring commissions, boards and other deliberatory bodies to hold open meetings — "meetings in the sunshine." The idea is that open meetings will provide transparency to government decision making and boost citizens' confidence in the decisions of deliberative bodies. Public understanding of the basis for decisions will hopefully be increased by open discussion, while fears of back room deals will be reduced if the door to the room is wide open.

Sunshine requirements are subject to various exceptions, including, for example, discussions of some personnel matters and contract issues.

The requirements of the many statutes vary considerably. For example, what kinds of bodies are covered? Are advisory committees or only bodies with actual decisional authority? What constitutes a meeting, which must be open? Must there be enough participating commissioners to make a quorum? Are emails, email list serves, or chat-rooms involving multiple board members to be treated as "meetings"— which must be open to the public? How would they be opened? What about conference calls? Are they meetings and must they be noticed and open to the public? Are pre-decisional discussions covered? These issues have been addressed differently in different jurisdictions.

To some observers, the sunshine laws have created more problems than they have solved. In particular, many observers and some members of commissions have complained that open meetings stifle open discussions. Members may be reluctant to engage in public exchanges of ideas, particularly novel ideas, if they are fearful that unpolished comments will be taken out of context or will be criticized for not reflecting ideas that are fully formed. Yet much constructive dialogue is built upon exchanges of preliminary ideas and questions. The concern is that deliberative bodies cannot fulfill their full potential if their members are discouraged from fully deliberating.

Some bodies have worked around the problems by circulating drafts and voting notationally, by meeting in numbers below the number that triggers the sunshine meeting requirement, by shifting discussions to professional staff advisors whose meetings are not covered by the open meeting rules, and by email exchanges in states which permit them. It is by no means clear that decision making has been enhanced or that imagined corruption has been stifled.

Whether or not you like the sunshine rules, they are a fact of life. Most deliberative bodies covered by the rules have adapted to the sunshine reality and make an effort to educate and re-educate members how to comply. Often the guidance is found in opinion letters from a state Attorney General or the legal advisor to a board, rather than in court decisions.

Since many lawyers and business people are brought into advisory committees or boards, you may find yourself or a client subjected to the sunshine laws of your particular state. Or, you may find you have to deal with the sunshine and advisory committee requirements at the federal level. Either way, as a lawyer dealing with administrative law, you may well find yourself advising a client on how to comply with sunshine laws or formulating guidelines for yourself.

EXERCISE 16A — SUNSHINE RULES FOR AN ADVISORY BOARD

A client tells you that he has been appointed to an important advisory board by the Governor of your home State. The advisory board is known as the Property Assessment Policy Board. Its nine members will advise the Governor and Legislature about how to reform the State's system for assessing commercial property. Your client owns numerous commercial buildings either in his own name or through partnerships he has with other investors. The advisory committee is tasked to draft a policy and legislative language on the subject. It will have the assistance of professional staff members from the State's Department of Taxation. Its work will result in a report to the Governor and the Legislature.

Your client asks you to look at your home State's sunshine and disclosure laws to answer the following questions. (If you would rather choose another State — or if your home State does not have a sunshine law applicable to advisory boards — you are welcome to have your client be appointed by another State's governor and answer for that State. If you are working in a group with other students, be sure to arrange for a diversity of jurisdictions so you can compare your findings.)

1. Does your State have a sunshine law?

2. Does it apply to advisory committees or boards, such as the one to which your client has been appointed?

3. Does the sunshine law or other statute set forth any disclosure or conflict of interest provisions that might affect your client?

4. How many members of a nine-member advisory committee may meet to discuss the committee's business before their discussion is considered a meeting which must be open to the public?

5. What are the statute's requirements for announcing a meeting that is to be covered by the sunshine act's open meeting requirements?

6. If five members of the advisory committee are also members of another group, such as the local chamber of commerce, can they discuss the advisory committee's deliberations in that other group's meeting? Would that meeting need to be subject to an open-meeting notice?

7. Can individual members of the committee discuss the committee's business by phone or exchanges of email? How many participants in such a discussion will it take to trigger a public meeting requirement?

8. What about communicating with other board members through an electronic chat-room or an email list serve? What about using blind "CCs" of emails to reach more members than could meet in person?

9. If you have further questions, with which government official or office might you consult for reliable guidance?

When you are done compiling answers, discuss and compare your answers with other students in the class. Such discussions will help convey the diversity of rules in the various jurisdictions.

As you approach answering these questions, you may find useful sources in addition to the traditional legal research tools. A state office or official, such as your state Attorney General, may have posted advice to state officials and advisory board members about how to comply with applicable state sunshine laws. Such official pronouncements are probably authoritative. There may be judicial decisions as well, and they are certainly authoritative.

In addition, there are several useful websites by open-government advocates which can direct you to applicable state laws and policies. These would not be authoritative enough to be a basis for legal advice, but they may offer you a short-cut to finding the answers. Note also that, as examples, the LEXISNEXIS WEBCOURSE has Virginia's Sunshine Act, as well as a number of other documents, relevant to the issues raised above.

PART FIVE

COMPLEX ISSUES

OVERVIEW

Administrative law problems usually do not present themselves as discreet, single issue cases. They often are intertwined with other administrative law and regulatory issues, requiring you to call on a combination of the skills you have been developing as you work through this book. You may find yourself considering multiple issues as well as utilizing various administrative law tools, such as a FOIA request, to help develop your case.

Moreover, there are ways to approach agency personnel for guidance which do not exist in a judicial setting. This is important because, given the complexity of complying with some regulatory requirements, there often are compliance issues that warrant informal discussions to obtain guidance from an agency whether or not anything is formally filed. Indeed, in some instances, there may be no formal administrative law solution at hand other than informal discussions with the agency involved.

Finally, there are always new issues emerging which push the boundaries of administrative law and require its application in new contexts such as public/private partnerships. The purpose of the exercises that follow is to explore some of these informal and complex contexts.

Chapter 17

GETTING GUIDANCE FROM AN ADMINISTRATIVE AGENCY

ESTIMATED TIME FOR COMPLETION: 90 minutes

ESTIMATED LEVEL OF DIFFICULTY: Difficult

Introduction

Counseling clients concerning their regulatory risks and obligations is one of the central roles played by a private practitioner or in-house lawyer. Issues raised by clients will range from the fairly clear-cut to the very difficult. As in any area of law, you will answer those questions based, in the first instance, upon your experience and your reading of relevant statutes, court decisions, and the agency's own regulations, decisions, and guidance documents. Some of the potential guidance documents include interpretive orders, statements of policy, preambles to regulations, staff opinions, and staff manuals.

As with other areas of law, the consequences of error by you or your client can range from minor to major. At the low end, one may be required to come into compliance prospectively or correct past omissions. At the other end, a regulated entity could face investigations, fines, loss of a project or a license to do business, or a much higher level of scrutiny and regulation than your client wants to live with.

Fortunately, unlike other areas of law, you can often go beyond your own research and analysis and reach out to the agency for guidance on how a law or regulation applies to your client currently or under a hypothetical set of facts. Each agency has its own methods of answering inquiries, but here is a rough compendium of the commonly available options.

1. ***Talking to the agency staff.*** You may be able to get comfort, particularly on minor compliance issues and issues that have arisen before, simply by speaking to an agency staff member with relevant experience and responsibility. Obviously, the more senior the individual and the more settled the issue, the

more reliable will be the answer. Potential advantages to this approach are that you may be able to get a quick guidance and you may be able to get such guidance without disclosing your client's name. On the other hand, the agency is not legally bound by informal advice, which is generally oral anyway. Such consultation might help to defend against later charges that you client flagrantly or intentionally violated a regulation, but it will not afford complete protection from agency action. In any event, it is critical that you have accurately described the facts and that you have comfort that the individual will confirm that he gave the advice you later cite.

2. ***Seeking a written opinion from the agency staff***. An opinion from the agency's staff could be helpful and might be easier to get than a full agency opinion. Seeking such an opinion would clearly show that you were diligent in trying to find the right answer. The inquiry will have to be in writing and fully disclose relevant facts, likely including the client's identity. However, the agency is not bound by a written staff opinion, even if issued by its general counsel, and neither the staff nor the general counsel is likely to give a clear answer unless the question has a well-settled answer. Still, relying upon such advice will probably insulate your client from much later criticism even if the agency ultimately rules the other way.

3. ***Seeking a no-action letter***. A no-action letter advises your client that the agency staff will not bring an enforcement action or seek to penalize your client if your client undertakes activities that are accurately and fully described in your written inquiry. However, a staff no-action letter is a staff opinion expressed to a particular party based upon a particular set of facts described in the request for a no-action letter. It is not a formal agency rule or order, and it does not formally bind the agency. While your client will not get in trouble if it relies on a no-action letter from the agency staff — assuming the facts described in the written request are complete and accurate — the letter will not preclude the agency from announcing a different interpretation of law at a later time. Furthermore, a no-action letter will not control private lawsuits. Thus, the value of a no-action letter will vary according to the circumstances. If your client desires assurance that it will never be subject to an agency's regulation, a no-action letter may not have the desired result: if the agency changes its interpretation of the scope so that it applies to entities like your client, the no-action letter will simply mean that your client will not be criticized for not complying with the regulation sooner.

4. ***Seeking a declaratory order***. A declaratory order is issued by the agency itself. Consequently, unlike a staff opinion, it will be an authoritative decision by the agency. Not only will such a decision be binding (at least until the facts change), but it may be possible to obtain judicial review of an unfavorable order. A request for a declaratory order will disclose your client's identity, and protection afforded by the order will only be as good as the accuracy of your filing's portrayal of the facts.

5. ***Seeking a waiver or exemption***. If you believe that your client is subject to a given set of regulatory requirements, you may need to file a petition for a

waiver or for an exemption. To do so, you will need to apply on behalf of a specific client and clearly to disclose all relevant facts, the problem it faces, and the scope of the proposed waiver. You will need to persuasively argue why an exemption or waiver would serve — or at least not harm — the public interest. Perhaps your client has some unique characteristics which would permit an exemption or a modified form of compliance while still achieving the overall goals of applicable regulations. Or, perhaps it is seeking a waiver for a past period in which it was out of compliance.

6. ***Petitioning for a rulemaking.*** Depending upon the agency and the regulatory circumstances, your only option may be to seek to modify an applicable regulation. Denial of a petition for a rulemaking is likely to be judicially reviewable, but inaction may not be reviewable.

Your choice of options will be driven by a variety of factors, including the procedural options available from the specific agency, your client's need for certainty, its current level of uncertainty, the consequences to your client from making a regulatory mistake, and the timing it needs for an answer. If you are pretty sure of the answer and the staff gives you an oral confirmation, you may be very comfortable with advising a client, subject to the usual qualifications (current law and policy, assumed facts, etc.), that it is safe to proceed. On the other hand, if you think it is a close call and the consequences of an error would be severe, you and your client will likely want to seek a higher level of assurance that the agency agrees with your interpretation of the law and regulations. Remember, also, that you are not necessarily limited to one option. You might, for example, informally consult the agency staff by a phone call or meeting in order to identify the most appropriate way to obtain formal guidance your client can reasonably rely upon.

The one common theme in any request for guidance is that you need to be completely candid and accurate about the facts and very clear what your question is. If you are vague or misleading, then the advice you receive will be of no value at all. An agency will happily walk away from any advice given in response to misrepresentations about the relevant facts, and it might penalize the lawyer and his client for their misrepresentations.

There are three hypotheticals set forth below. For each, you should evaluate the hypothetical and analyze which of the forms of guidance you would recommend that the client seek. Write a brief memo setting forth your recommended course of action, the issue you would seek to have answered, and the reason for recommending that course of action. Note that the LEXISNEXIS WEBCOURSE includes various examples of guidance documents from federal agencies.

EXERCISE 17A — FINDING EXAMPLES OF AGENCY GUIDANCE

Review at least two of the following websites for examples of guidance documents and for guidelines for obtaining guidance. Most federal regulatory agencies will have similar web pages discussing compliance guidance.

Securities and Exchange Commission: www.sec.gov

> Staff guidance: http://www.sec.gov/interps.shtml

> Division of Investment Management (page of website):
> http://www.sec.gov/divisions/investment.shtml

Environmental Protection Agency: www.epa.gov

> Compliance: http://www.epa.gov/lawsregs/compliance/

Federal Energy Regulatory Commission

> "Interpretive Order Modifying No-Action Letter Process and Reviewing Other Mechanisms for Obtaining Guidance," 123 FERC 61,157 (2008) (Docket PL08-2-000).

Department of Labor: www.dol.gov

> Compliance assistance: http://www.dol.gov/compliance/

> Exemptions for a class or individual:
> http://www.dol.gov/ebsa/regs/technical_guidance.html#exemptions

> Information letters: http://www.dol.gov/ebsa/Regs/ILs/main.html

> Advisory opinions: http://www.dol.gov/ebsa/Regs/AOs/main.html

> Field assistance bulletins: http://www.dol.gov/ebsa/Regs/fabmain.html

> Technical releases: http://www.dol.gov/ebsa/regs/main.html#technicalreleases

EXERCISE 17B — GETTING AGENCY ADVICE

Your client is a bank (Seventh Southwest National). It has negotiated to lend money to a water company (Wonder Water) to build a new pumping station. The idea is for the bank to own the pumping station and to lease it to the water company under a 20-year lease. The term of the lease matches the term of the loan and the lease payments equate to the loan payments. The bank's idea is that by retaining ownership, it would be easier to preserve the asset and to remove and resell the pump in the event of a default or in the event of bankruptcy. The bank has no intention of taking responsibility for operating the water system. However, the lease agreement requires Wonder Water to maintain the pumping station according to accepted industry standards, which the bank can enforce through audit and arbitration provisions in the agreement. Also, the bank could remove the pump in the event of a default, which would obviously undermine Wonder Water's ability to provide service required by Wonder Water's utility obligations.

The applicable State water law provides, in relevant part:

Section 1. Each owner and operator of a water delivery system located in whole or part within the State shall be regulated by the Public Service Commission as a public utility.

Section 4. No public utility shall terminate service except pursuant to the terms of regulations or orders issued by the Public Service Commission.

Section 5. All public utilities shall charge just and reasonable rates approved by the Public Service Commission. To facilitate such rate regulation and to assure financial health of all utilities, each public utility shall submit an annual report and quarterly reports setting forth such detailed corporate and financial data as is requested by the Public Service Commission and shall be subject to audit by the Public Service Commission.

Seventh Southwest would like the added security of retaining ownership as a "security interest" for its loan, but it cannot afford to become a regulated public utility. Subjecting the bank to regulation as a "public utility" would devastate the company and the bank's president could lose his job. Although you can find examples in other jurisdictions, your research finds no case in your State in which a lender holds title to essential utility equipment which it leases to a public utility. You find one decision in which your State Public Service Commission opined that a passive ownership interest might not subject a company to public utility regulation, but the discussion was dictum. The author of a treatise on public utility law has explicitly stated, based on the law in other States, that your State Public Service Commission should not regulate a passive owner as a public utility.

Assuming that all the options outlined at the beginning of the chapter are available, how would you advise the client to proceed? Outline your advice and reasoning in a letter to your client.

EXERCISE 17C — ADVISING A CLIENT ON A VIOLATION

It is now three years since the FEA promulgated its regulations concerning emissions of Methyloxystuff. Those regulations include a requirement that all emitters file annual and quarterly reports concerning their emissions and their implementation of measures to limit emissions.

Your client, Chemicals Galore, produces Methyloxystuff, as it has for many years. You have discovered in the course of discussions with your client that Chemicals Galore has not made the annual and quarterly filings that FEA mandates for all emitters of Methyloxystuff.

The FEA form for the annual report requires the reporting party to state whether it filed all required reports during the prior 24 months and, if not, to identify the missing reports and to explain why it failed to do so. The next annual report is due to be filed in two months. Violations of the statute and applicable regulations can result in penalties of up to $100,000 per violation.

How would you advise Client X to proceed? Outline your advice to your client about how it should proceed. Your client will want a written memorandum; but, initially, it wants to hear your advice. If you are working with a classmate, you might have him or her play the role of client, answering your questions and asking you questions about your advice.

Chapter 18

INFORMAL EMERGENCY ACTION

ESTIMATED TIME FOR COMPLETION: 60 minutes

ESTIMATED LEVEL OF DIFFICULTY: Moderate

Formal adjudicatory and informal rulemaking procedures apply to a very small percentage of the decisions made by administrative agencies. It is estimated that approximately 90% are made informally where neither adjudicatory or rulemaking procedures apply. And, many times, adjudicatory procedures written into an agency's own enabling act may not be available due to a perceived emergency involved. The exercise below explores a situation where it is not likely that any formal adjudicatory procedures can be invoked in a timely manner but where agency action may, nevertheless, be necessary.

EXERCISE 18A — REGULATION BY PUBLICITY

Under the provisions of the Federal Meat Inspection Act, 21 U.S.C. § 601 *et seq.*, the Department of Agriculture is empowered to police the safety of most of this country's beef supply by creating rules to regulate the processing of beef, by monitoring compliance with these regulations at meat processing plants, and by inspecting and grading beef produced in meat processing plants. Section 673 of the Act also empowers the USDA to institute an *in rem* action in U.S. District Court where beef is found that fails to conform to the standards of the Act. Any party to this proceeding may request a trial by jury.

One power that Congress did *not* give the USDA is the power to order a meat processor to recall beef that has already been shipped into the stream of commerce — for example, that which has been sold to grocery stores. *In rem* actions to seize beef are relatively rare; typically, the meat processor will engage in negotiations with the USDA as to the potential scope of the problem and will voluntarily recall the tainted beef. If these negotiations break down, the USDA can stop inspecting further meat produced at the plant, which has the effect of shutting down the facility, and/or initiating the *in rem* actions to condemn the beef in the stream of commerce.

On December 9, a cow was slaughtered at the Vern's Moses Lake Meats slaughter house, located on a farm in the State of Washington. Tissues were taken from one cow and tested — two weeks later the USDA determined that the cow tested positively for mad cow disease. Thirteen other cows were also slaughtered that day at Vern's Moses Lake Meats slaughter house. When the USDA got confirmation of this two weeks later they immediately quarantined the farm but became worried about how widespread the distribution of possibly tainted beef already may have been. Moses Meats ships to grocery stores in Alaska, Washington, Oregon, Arizona, and New Mexico. The Secretary asks you what she can do now.

Assume you are an attorney in the USDA and in response to the Secretary's question, you express your concern that the USDA will not be able to obtain a preliminary injunction against the sale of the beef in every district court in which it might bring suit because of the admitted "extremely low likelihood" that the most of the beef contained the agent that causes mad cow disease. Similarly, you conclude that *in rem* proceedings are not practical because they would take too long. You recommend the agency issue a press release that — "out of an abundance of caution" — informs the general public of the possible dangers that might exist and warns that consumers should not eat any meat that came from Vern's Moses Meats or might have been contaminated by that meat. Vern's Moses Meats did not, however, keep detailed records of which lot of beef went to which grocery outlets.

Could the USDA issue a press release such as this warning everyone in all of the states likely to be affected?

> The Federal Meat Inspection Act, 21 U.S.C. §§ 601, 673 deals with *in rem* actions. Section 673(a)(1) states:
>
>> Any carcass, part of a carcass, meat or food product . . . that is being transported in commerce or . . . and that (A) is or has been prepared, sold, transported, or otherwise distributed or offered or received for distribution

in violation of this chapter, or (B) is capable of use as human food and is adulterated or misbranded, or (C) in any other way is in violation of this chapter, shall be liable to be proceeded against and seized and condemned, at any time, on a libel of information in any United States district court or other proper court as provided in section 674 of this title within the jurisdiction of which the article or animal is found.

Can you infer from this provision that the Agency has the power to issue a press release warning consumers of the dangers of a tainted meat supply when an *in rem* proceeding is impractical? How would you advise the Secretary about the appropriateness of issuing a press release identifying the tainted meat supply and its source?

EXERCISE 18B — DEFENDING THE CLIENT

Assume you are the attorney representing Vern's Moses Meats. Are you willing to go along with the USDA's suggestion that you voluntarily recall the beef distributed on and after December 9? What are your legal rights? How much negotiating room do you have?

EXERCISE 18C- DRAFTING THE PRESS RELEASE

Draft the press release that you think will effectively protect the public interest and enlist the cooperation of Vern's Moses Meats. Assume that you have been in touch with Vern's attorney and that you and he negotiated the wording of that press release. What do you think it should look like?

Chapter 19

PRIVATIZATION AND THE OUTSOURCING OF AGENCY RESPONSIBILITIES: THE MANAGEMENT OF FEDERAL PRISONS

ESTIMATED TIME FOR COMPLETION: 90 minutes

ESTIMATED LEVEL OF DIFFICULTY: Difficult

Outsourcing is a common form of privatization in the United States — contracting out what were once exclusively government-provided services to the private sector. A key question that arises is whether certain governmental functions should be regarded as "inherently governmental" and thus precluded from outsourcing. If, however, the conclusion is that the functions in question are not inherently governmental, are the contracts that are then entered into between the private providers and the outsourcing agency subject to any public processes? Would, for example, the notice and comment procedures of the APA apply? And does the Freedom of Information Act, apply to private entities carrying out public functions? The exercises that follow will explore these and other aspects of agency outsourcing.

EXERCISE 19A — CHALLENGING PRIVITIZATION

Assume that Inmates We Trust, an inmates' advocacy group, has recently learned that the Federal Bureau of Prisons ("BOP"), an agency within the Department of Justice, plans to outsource the management of a federal prison in Illinois to a private firm. Inmates We Trust is concerned that privatizing the management of this federal prison will decrease the quality of prison life as well as make it more difficult to ensure that prisoners' rights are respected. Indeed, in just the last few years, the group has received a number of complaints from inmates at other private prisons. Last month, the BOP gave formal notice of the competitive bidding process to privatize the prison in Illinois.

Inmates We Trust ask you to be their attorney and to do whatever you can to block this privatization effort. You learn that all agency outsourcing proposals in the federal government must pass through the Office of Management and Budget (OMB). The OMB's Circular A-76 governs the privatization procedure. Go to the OMB's website (http://www.whitehouse.gov/omb/circulars_default/) and find this Circular.

(a) Does it provide any way for your client to provide any input at this stage of the decision making process? Can you bring a law suit on behalf of your client attempting to stop this decision to outsource? On what grounds?

(b) Once a decision is made to contract with a certain firm, are there any procedures that can make the contract negotiation process with the private provider a transparent one? Do APA informal rulemaking procedures apply?

EXERCISE 19B — LIMITS ON PRIVITIZATION

After researching the issue, you further discover that the OMB will only approve agency privatization measures if they are in accord with the requirements of the Federal Activities Inventory Reform Act of 1998 ("the Fair Act"), 112 Stat. 2382. The Fair Act mandates that no "inherently governmental function" may be outsourced to private industry. The statute defines it as follows:

(2) Inherently governmental function. —

    (A) Definition. — The term "inherently governmental function" means a function that is so intimately related to the public interest as to require performance by Federal Government employees.

    (B) Functions included. — The term includes activities that require either the exercise of discretion in applying Federal Government authority or the making of valuable judgments in making decisions for the Federal Government, including judgments relating to monetary transactions and entitlements. An inherently governmental function involves, among other things, the interpretation and execution of the laws of the United States so as —

    (i) to bind the United States to take or not to take some action by contract, policy, regulation, authorization, order, or otherwise;

    (ii) to determine, protect, and advance United States economic, political, territorial, property, or other interest by military or diplomatic action, civil or criminal judicial proceedings, contract management or otherwise;

    (iii) to significantly affect the life, liberty, or property of private persons;

    (iv) to commission, appoint, direct, or control officers or employees of the United States; or

    (v) to exert ultimate control over the acquisition, use, or disposition of the property, real or personal, tangible or intangible, of the United States, including the collection, control, or disbursement of appropriated and other Federal funds.

    (C) Functions excluded. — The term does not normally include —

    (i) gathering information for or providing advice, opinions, recommendations, or ideas to Federal Government officials; or

    (ii) any function that is primarily ministerial and internal in nature (such as building security, mail operations, operation of cafeterias, housekeeping, facilities operations and maintenance, warehouse operations, motor vehicle fleet management operations, or other routine electrical or mechanical services).

Prepare a memo that explores whether there are any statutory or constitutional limits to what can be outsourced in a federal prison context? Can the day-to-day management of the facility be outsourced? Can its construction? Are there constitutional limits if a private provider hires private judges to adjudicate disputes, the outcome of which might mean a longer sentence of the inmate involved? Who can raise these issues and how might they go about it?

EXERCISE 19C: PRISONER HEALTH CARE

Assume that the BOP went ahead and outsourced the management of this prison to a private corporation, FreeMarket Prison Solutions, Inc. Under the terms of FreeMarket's contract with BOP, it is responsible for the administration and maintenance of the prison, as well as for supervising, disciplining, and caring for the health of its inmates. Its contract with BOP authorizes it to subcontract out for any services it cannot provide itself. To that end it subcontracted with another private company, Health Services Inc., for the provision of health care services for the prisoners. This includes tending to the physical, dental, and mental health care needs of the inmates.

You have agreed to represent an inmate at this prison. Your client claims that FreeMarket has failed, on numerous occasions, to tend to many of his basic health care needs, as well as those of other inmates. He claims that not only is FreeMarket slow to bring physicians in to see patients, but the company is unlikely to take inmates medical complaints seriously. In fact, your client, after complaining repeatedly to guards and prison authorities of a severe toothache — all of which went unheeded — got a fever. By the time prison officials brought physicians in to tend to your client and realized that his rotten tooth was the cause of his illness, his tooth, along with several surrounding teeth, required pulling. Your client still has severe pain in his mouth from scarring caused by his infected tooth.

Three exercises follow from these facts:

EXERCISE 19C (1) — THIRD PARTY BENEFICIARY?

Your client asks you to bring a suit against FreeMarket and the BOP on his behalf, alleging that the contract under which FreeMarket operates has been breached. Can you bring such a suit arguing that your client is a third-party beneficiary of this contract? In determining who is and is not a third-party beneficiary, the Restatement (Second) of Contracts is instructive:

§ 302:

(1)   Unless otherwise agreed between promisor and promise, a beneficiary of a promise is an intended beneficiary if recognition of a right to performance in the beneficiary is appropriate to effectuate the intention of the parties either

   (a)   The performance of the promise will satisfy an obligation of the promise to pay money to the beneficiary; or

   (b)   The circumstances indicate that the promise intends to give the beneficiary the benefit of the promised performance.

(2)   An incidental beneficiary is a beneficiary who is not an intended beneficiary.

   (a)   If not, who has standing to sue? In answering the third-party beneficiary question, take a look at *Astra USA, Inc. v. Santa Clara*, 563 U.S. ___ (2011) (slip opinion), which is on the **LEXISNEXIS WEBCOURSE**. Also, for purposes of making your argument, take a look at Rathke v. Corrections Corp. of America, 153 P.3d 303 (Alaska 2007).

   (b)   If you conclude that a federal prisoner is not a third-party beneficiary, how can the contract for medical services be enforced? Are there any informal remedies to explore? Go to the agency's webpage (www.bop.gov) to locate BOP's rules or regulations for remedies. Click on the tab for "Policy/Forms," then on "Find a Policy." Click then on "Browse Series" next to "Administrative and Management." Search within Program 1330.16, "Administrative Remedy Program."

EXERCISE 19C (2) — USING FOIA

Suppose you wish to file a FOIA request to obtain information about the number of doctors available to these prisoners as well as other details of their care and the staff available to them. To whom do you make this request? What do you ask for? How do you frame your request?

EXERCISE 19C (3) — STRIKING A BALANCE

As a public interest organization focused on prisoner rights, what changes would you like to make in existing laws in order to enhance public oversight and protection of prisoners, given that prison privatization is now so pervasive at the state and federal levels of government?

Chapter 20

TSA NO FLY LISTS

ESTIMATED TIME FOR COMPLETION: 60 minutes

ESTIMATED LEVEL OF DIFFICULTY: Moderate

Following the September 11, 2001 terrorist attacks, the United States government identified as a major national security liability the vulnerability of airlines operating within national airspace. In the hopes of shoring up security, Congress passed a law mandating, unifying, and increasing airport-screening procedures. The law requires that the Transportation Security Administration (TSA), an agency of the Department of Homeland Security, ensure that passengers are not "carrying unlawfully a dangerous weapon, explosive, or other destructive substance." 49 U.S.C. § 44901(a). Congress left it to the agency, however, to prescribe the details of the screening process. The TSA has set forth its regulations in a set of Standard Operating Procedures (SOP) not available to the public. In addition to the SOPs, the agency has promulgated a blanket regulation barring any person who has not been screened by TSA from entering the so-called "sterile area" of an airport, the area on the departure side of the screening machines.

The ACLU recently received a call from a Virginia man, whose son — a U.S. citizen — has been unable to reenter the country. Your supervising attorney assigns the case to you, with the hopes that you can help the man and his son.

The Virginia man was born in Saudi Arabia, but has since become a naturalized U.S. citizen. His son, Jamil, was born in the United States, and holds passports for both the U.S. and Saudi Arabia.

Jamil, traveling in Saudi Arabia for the Haj — the annual pilgrimage to Mecca — was arrested by unknown assailants after attending prayers led by a well-known Imam, Salman Al Aouda. Al Aouda is widely thought to condone extreme Islamist groups throughout the Persian Gulf, and indeed, was rumored to have helped finance the 2003 terrorist bombings in Madrid, Spain.

After his arrest, Jamil was blindfolded and thrown into a van. He was taken to a facility where he endured brutal interrogation techniques. They asked him about his association with Al Aouda; they spoke in both Arabic and American English. He denied any association with the Imam, other than attending that lone prayer meeting. Due to the techniques used, Jamil showed no external injuries. After keeping him overnight, he was again blindfolded, thrown into a van, and driven to King Khalid International Airport at dawn. They removed his blindfold him and as the van was still moving, pushed him to the street; he never saw, and thus, could not identify his captors. They placed only his two passports and his return airline ticket in his front pocket.

Intimidated, he attempted to board the next plane for the United States. At the airline's check-in, he was told that his ticket was not processing and that he should wait in the airport's main foyer. Using a payphone, he called his father to tell him what happened. After three hours of waiting, four security guards approached him, forced him to his feet, and escorted him from the building. He was allowed to fly back to the United States under the supervision of a U. S. Sky Marshall. He subsequently learned, however, that he had been placed on the U.S. No Fly List.

The No Fly List is generated by the Terrorist Screening Center (TSC), part of the Federal Bureau of Investigations (FBI). The FBI, in turn, is directly run by the Department of Justice (DOJ), headed by Attorney General Eric H. Holder, Jr. In its counterterrorism efforts, the TSC develops and maintains the federal government's consolidated Terrorist Screening Database (TSDB) of which the No Fly List is a component.

The TSC was established by President Bush in his Homeland Security Presidential Directive-6, which directed TSC to "consolidate the Government's approach to terrorism screening and provide for the appropriate and lawful use of Terrorist Information in screening processes." While the TSC creates, maintains, and controls its TSDB, in the context of air travel, when individuals make airline reservations and check in at airports, the front-line screening agency, the Transportation Security Administration (TSA), and the commercial airline, conduct a name-based search of the individual to determine whether he or she is on the TSDB.

Only two government entities have the authority to nominate individuals for inclusion in the TSDB: the FBI and the National Counterterrorism Center (NCTC). NCTC, a part of the Office of the Director of National Intelligence, relies on information from other federal departments and agencies when including known or suspected international terrorists in its Terrorist Identities Datamart Environment (TIDE) database. The NCTC identifies international terrorists; the FBI identifies domestic threats. While both the FBI and NCTC may nominate names for the TSDB, the TSC makes the final decision as to whether a nominated individual meets the minimum requirements for inclusion on the list.

The TSC does not, itself, have any redress procedures for disputing one's name on the No Fly List. The Department of Homeland Security, however, does, in its Department of Homeland Security Traveler Redress Inquiry Program (DHS TRIP). While the TSA may make a request to the TSC to review a name on the list, the TSC is under no obligation by statute to cooperate with the DHS TRIP process. Find the DHS TRIP program.

Go to the Department of Homeland Security's website (www.dhs.gov) and select "File a travel complaint" on the right. Does this resolve any due process concerns Jamil may have? Should he file a travel complaint?

EXERCISE 20A — DUE PROCESS

Assume that you represent Jamil. He ultimately was allowed to return to the United States but he remains on the No Fly List. You decide to file a complaint to be filed in Federal District Court on behalf of Jamil with the Justice Department, the FBI, and the TSC as defendants. What procedural due process issues will you raise? Outline the key elements of that complaint.

EXERCISE 20B — IDENTIFYING CONTRARY ARGUMENTS

What arguments do you expect will be made in opposition to your complaint? What are your chances of succeeding on your claims? If you were the judge in this case, how would you rule?

Appendix

HOMERSVILLE — NORTH CENTRAL EXERCISES

For Use with Chapters 1-5

STATUTORY MATERIALS

Natural Gas Act (excerpts)

Endangered Species Act (excerpts)

CASE MATERIALS

Application by North Central Gas Pipeline Company

FERC Notice of Application

Protest, Motion to Intervene and Request for Hearing of The Homersville Audubon Society

Summary of other protests

Excerpts from Natural Gas Act, Title 15 U.S.C. 717 (highlighted)

§ 717. Regulation of natural gas companies

(b) Transactions to which provisions of chapter applicable

The provisions of this chapter shall apply to the transportation of natural gas in interstate commerce, to the sale in interstate commerce of natural gas for resale for ultimate public consumption for domestic, commercial, industrial, or any other use, and to natural-gas companies engaged in such transportation or sale, . . . but shall not apply to any other transportation or sale of natural gas or to the local distribution of natural gas or to the facilities used for such distribution or to the production or gathering of natural gas . . . .

§ 717a. Definitions (NGA Section 2)

When used in this chapter, unless the context otherwise requires —

. . . .

(5) "Natural gas" means either natural gas unmixed, or any mixture of natural and artificial gas.

(6) **"Natural-gas company" means a person engaged in the transportation of natural gas in interstate commerce, or the sale in interstate commerce of such gas for resale.**

(7) "Interstate commerce" means commerce between any point in a State and any point outside thereof, or between points within the same State but through any place outside thereof, but only insofar as such commerce takes place within the United States.

. . . .

(9) "Commission" and "Commissioner" means the [Federal Energy Regulatory Commission, formerly the Federal Power Commission], and a member thereof, respectively.

§ 717f.   Construction, extension, or abandonment of facilities (NGA Section 7)

. . . .

(c)   **Certificate of public convenience and necessity**

(1) (A)   **No natural-gas company** or person which will be a natural-gas company upon completion of any proposed construction or extension **shall engage in the transportation or sale of natural gas, subject to the jurisdiction of the Commission, or undertake the construction or extension of any facilities therefor, or acquire or operate any such facilities or extensions thereof, unless there is in force with respect to such natural-gas company a certificate of public convenience and necessity issued by the Commission authorizing such acts or operations . . . .**

(B)   **In all . . . cases [other than pipelines existing prior to enactment] the Commission shall set the matter for hearing and shall give such reasonable notice of the hearing thereon to all interested persons as in its judgment may be necessary under rules and regulations to be prescribed by the Commission; and the application shall be decided in accordance with the procedure provided in subsection (e) of this section and such certificate shall be issued or denied accordingly . . . .**

(d)   **Application for certificate of public convenience and necessity**

Application for certificates shall be made in writing to the Commission, be verified under oath, and shall be in such form, contain such information, and notice thereof shall be served upon such interested parties and in such manner as the Commission shall, by regulation, require.

(e)   **Granting of certificate of public convenience and necessity**

. . . [A] **certificate shall be issued to any qualified applicant therefor, authorizing the whole or any part of the operation, sale, service, construction, extension, or acquisition covered by the application, if it is found that the applicant is able and willing properly to do the acts and to perform the service proposed and to conform to the provisions of this chapter and the requirements, rules, and regulations of the Commission thereunder, and that the proposed service, sale, operation, construction, extension, or acquisition, to the extent authorized by the certificate, is or will be required by the present or future public convenience and necessity; otherwise such application shall be denied. The Commission shall have the power to attach to the issuance of the certificate and to the exercise of the rights granted thereunder such reasonable terms and conditions as the public convenience and necessity may require.**

. . .

(h)   **Right of eminent domain for construction of pipelines, etc.**

When any holder of a certificate of public convenience and necessity cannot acquire by contract, or is unable to agree with the owner of property to the compensation to be paid for, the necessary right-of-way to construct, operate, and maintain a pipe line or pipe lines for the transportation of natural gas, and the necessary land or other property, in addition to right-of-way, . . . it may acquire the same by the exercise of the right of eminent domain in the district court of the United States for the district in which such property may be located, or in the State courts. . . .

§ 717n.   Process coordination; hearings; rules of procedure (NGA Section 15)

(a)   **Definition**

In this section, the term **"Federal authorization"** —

   (1) means any authorization required under Federal law with respect to an application for . . . a certificate of public convenience and necessity under section 717f of this title; and

   (2) includes any permits, special use authorizations, certifications, opinions, or other approvals as may be required under Federal law with respect to . . . a certificate of public convenience and necessity under section 717f of this title.

(b)   **Designation as lead agency**

   (1)   **In general**

The Commission shall act as the lead agency for the purposes of coordinating all applicable Federal authorizations and for the purposes of complying with the National Environmental Policy Act of 1969 (42 U.S.C. 4321 et seq.).

   (2)   **Other agencies**

Each Federal and State agency considering an aspect of an application for Federal authorization shall cooperate with the Commission and comply with the deadlines established by the Commission.

(c)   **Schedule**

   (1)   **Commission authority to set schedule**

The Commission shall establish a schedule for all Federal authorizations. In establishing the schedule, the Commission shall —

      (A) ensure expeditious completion of all such proceedings; and

      (B) comply with applicable schedules established by Federal law.

   (2)   **Failure to meet schedule**

If a Federal or State administrative agency does not complete a proceeding for an approval that is required for a Federal authorization in accordance with the schedule established by the Commission, the applicant may pursue remedies under section 717r (d) of this title.

(d) **Consolidated record**

The Commission shall, with the cooperation of Federal and State administrative agencies and officials, maintain a complete consolidated record of all decisions made or actions taken by the Commission or by a Federal administrative agency or officer (or State administrative agency or officer acting under delegated Federal authority) with respect to any Federal authorization. Such record shall be the record for —

. . .

(2) judicial review under section 717r (d) of this title of decisions made or actions taken of Federal and State administrative agencies and officials, provided that, if the Court determines that the record does not contain sufficient information, the Court may remand the proceeding to the Commission for further development of the consolidated record.

(e) **Hearings; parties**

Hearings under this chapter may be held before the Commission, any member or members thereof, or any representative of the Commission designated by it, and appropriate records thereof shall be kept. In any proceeding before it, the Commission in accordance with such rules and regulations as it may prescribe, may admit as a party any interested State, State commission, municipality or any representative of interested consumers or security holders, or any competitor of a party to such proceeding, or any other person whose participation in the proceeding may be in the public interest.

(f) **Procedure**

All hearings, investigations, and proceedings under this chapter shall be governed by rules of practice and procedure to be adopted by the Commission, and in the conduct thereof the technical rules of evidence need not be applied. No informality in any hearing, investigation, or proceeding or in the manner of taking testimony shall invalidate any order, decision, rule, or regulation issued under the authority of this chapter.

§ 717o. Administrative powers of Commission; rules, regulations, and orders (NGA Section 16)

The Commission shall have power to perform any and all acts, and to prescribe, issue, make, amend, and rescind such orders, rules, and regulations as it may find necessary or appropriate to carry out the provisions of this chapter . . . .

§ 717r. Rehearing and review (NGA Section 19)

(a) **Application for rehearing; time**

Any person, State, municipality, or State commission aggrieved by an order issued by the Commission in a proceeding under this chapter to which such person, State, municipality, or State commission is a party may apply for a rehearing within thirty days after the issuance of such order. The application for rehearing shall set forth specifically the ground or grounds upon which such application is based. Upon such application the Commission shall have power to grant or deny rehearing or to abrogate or modify its order without further hearing. Unless the Commission acts upon the application for rehearing within thirty days after it is filed, such application may be deemed to have been denied. **No proceeding to review any order of the Commission shall be brought by any person unless such person shall have made application to the Commission for a rehearing thereon . . . .**

(b) **Review of Commission order**

Any party to a proceeding under this chapter aggrieved by an order issued by the Commission in such proceeding may obtain a review of such order in the court of appeals of the United States for any circuit wherein the natural-gas company to which the order relates is located or has its principal place of business, or in the United States Court of Appeals for the District of Columbia, by filing in such court, within sixty days after the order of the Commission upon the application for rehearing, a written petition praying that the order of the Commission be modified or set aside in whole or in part. A copy of such petition shall forthwith be transmitted by the clerk of the court to any member of the Commission and thereupon the Commission shall file with the court the record upon which the order complained of was entered, as provided in section 2112 of title 28. Upon the filing of such petition such court shall have jurisdiction, which upon the filing of the record with it shall be exclusive, to affirm, modify, or set aside such order in whole or in part. **No objection to the order of the Commission shall be considered by the court unless such objection shall have been urged before the Commission in the application for rehearing unless there is reasonable ground for failure so to do. The finding of the Commission as to the facts, if supported by substantial evidence, shall be conclusive. If any party shall apply to the court for leave to adduce additional evidence, and shall show to the satisfaction of the court that such additional evidence is material and that there were reasonable grounds for failure to adduce such evidence in the proceedings before the Commission, the court may order such additional evidence to be taken before the Commission and to be adduced upon the hearing in such manner and upon such terms and conditions as to the court may seem proper.** The Commission may modify its findings as to the facts by reason of the additional evidence so taken, and it shall file with the court such modified or new findings, which is supported by substantial evidence, shall be conclusive, and its recommendation, if any, for the modification or setting aside of the original order. The judgment and decree of the court, affirming, modifying, or setting aside, in whole or in part, any such order of the Commission, shall be final, subject to review by the Supreme Court of the United States upon certiorari or certification as provided in section 1254 of title 28.

(c) **Stay of Commission order**

The filing of an application for rehearing under subsection (a) of this section shall not, unless specifically ordered by the Commission, operate as a stay of the Commission's order. The commencement of proceedings under subsection (b) of this section shall not, unless specifically ordered by the court, operate as a stay of the Commission's order.

EXCERPTS FROM THE ENDANGERED SPECIES ACT

USCA Title 16. Conservation, Chapter 35. Endangered Species

§ 1531. Congressional findings and declaration of purposes and policy

. . . .

(b) Purposes

The purposes of this chapter are to provide a means whereby the ecosystems upon which endangered species and threatened species depend may be conserved, to provide a program for the conservation of such endangered species and threatened species, and to take such steps as may be appropriate to achieve the purposes of the treaties and conventions set forth in subsection (a) of this section.

(c) Policy

(1) It is further declared to be the policy of Congress that all Federal departments and agencies shall seek to conserve endangered species and threatened species and shall utilize their authorities in furtherance of the purposes of this chapter.

(2) It is further declared to be the policy of Congress that Federal agencies shall cooperate with State and local agencies to resolve water resource issues in concert with conservation of endangered species.

. . . .

§ 1536. Interagency cooperation

(a) Federal agency actions and consultations

(1) The Secretary shall review other programs administered by him and utilize such programs in furtherance of the purposes of this chapter. All other Federal agencies shall, in consultation with and with the assistance of the Secretary, utilize their authorities in furtherance of the purposes of this chapter by carrying out programs for the conservation of endangered species and threatened species listed pursuant to section 1533 of this title.

(2) Each Federal agency shall, in consultation with and with the assistance of the Secretary, insure that any action authorized, funded, or carried out by such agency (hereinafter in this section referred to as an "agency action") is not likely to jeopardize the continued existence of any endangered species or threatened species or result in the destruction or adverse modification of habitat of such species which is determined by the Secretary, after consultation as appropriate with affected States, to be critical, unless such agency has been granted an exemption for such action by the Committee pursuant to subsection (h) of this section. In fulfilling the requirements of this paragraph each agency shall use the best scientific and commercial data available.

(3) Subject to such guidelines as the Secretary may establish, a Federal agency shall consult with the Secretary on any prospective agency action at the request of, and in cooperation with, the prospective permit or license applicant if the applicant has reason to believe that an endangered species or a threatened species may be present in the area affected by his project and that implementation of such action will likely affect such species.

(4) Each Federal agency shall confer with the Secretary on any agency action which is likely to jeopardize the continued existence of any species proposed to be listed under section 1533 of this title or result in the destruction or adverse modification of critical habitat proposed to be designated for such species. This paragraph does not require a limitation on the commitment of resources as described in subsection (d) of this section.

(b) Opinion of Secretary

. . . .

(3) (A) Promptly after conclusion of consultation under paragraph (2) or (3) of subsection (a) of this section, the Secretary shall provide to the Federal agency and the applicant, if any, a written statement setting forth the Secretary's opinion, and a summary of the information on which the opinion is based, detailing how the agency action affects the species or its critical habitat. If jeopardy or adverse modification is found, the Secretary shall suggest those reasonable and prudent alternatives which he believes would not violate subsection (a) (2) of this section and can be taken by the Federal agency or applicant in implementing the agency action.

. . . .

(c) Biological assessment

(1) To facilitate compliance with the requirements of subsection (a) (2) of this section, each Federal agency shall . . . request of the Secretary information whether any species which is listed or proposed to be listed may be present in the area of such proposed action. If the Secretary advises, based on the best scientific and commercial data available, that such species may be present, such agency shall conduct a biological assessment for the purpose of identifying any endangered species or threatened species which is likely to be affected by such action. . . . Such assessment may be undertaken as part of a Federal agency's compliance with the requirements of section 102 of the National Environmental Policy Act of 1969 (42 U.S.C. 4332).

. . . .

(d) Limitation on commitment of resources

After initiation of consultation required under subsection (a) (2) of this section, the Federal agency and the permit or license applicant shall not make any irreversible or irretrievable commitment of resources with respect to the agency action which has the effect of foreclosing the formulation or implementation of any reasonable and prudent alternative measures which would not violate subsection (a) (2) of this section.

UNITED STATES OF AMERICA
FEDERAL ENERGY REGULATORY COMMISSION

North Central Gas Pipeline Company   Docket No. CP11-6666-000

NOTICE OF REQUEST UNDER BLANKET AUTHORIZATION

(March 2, 2011)

Take notice that on February 31, 2011, North Central Gas Pipeline Company ("NORTH CENTRAL"), filed in the above-captioned docket pursuant to Sections 157.205 and 157.21 l(a)(2) of the Federal Energy Regulatory Commission's ("Commission") regulations under the Natural Gas Act, prior notice that it intends to construct, own and operate a delivery point to serve Fantastic Manufacturing Company ("Fantastic") located in Homersville, MN, as more fully set forth in the request which is on file with the Commission and open to public inspection.

NORTH CENTRAL proposes to construct, own and operate facilities necessary to deliver natural gas to serve Fantastic's manufacturing plant in Homersville, MN. NORTH CENTRAL proposes to install a 4-inch hot tap, a 1.2 mile 4-inch lateral delivery line, and related facilities connecting to its existing 16" pipeline. The new facilities will result in a bypass of the local distribution company operated by the Town of Homersville, which currently serves Fantastic. NORTH CENTRAL states that the proposed facilities will not have an impact upon NORTH CENTRAL's peak day deliveries and that it has sufficient capacity to render the transportation service without detriment to its existing customers.

Any questions regarding this request should be directed to Andre Gide, Vice President for Regulatory Affairs at the address and phone number set forth in the application.

This filing is available for review m the Commission or may be viewed on the Commission's web site at http://www.ferc.gov using the "eLibrary" link. Enter the docket number excluding the last three digits in the docket number field to access the document. For assistance, please contact FERC Online Support at FERCOnlineSupport@ferc.gov or toll free at (866) 208-3676, or for TTY, contact (202) 502-8659. Comments, protests and interventions may be filed electronically via the Internet in lieu of paper. See, 18 CFR 385.2001(a)(1)(iii) and the instructions on the Commission's web site under the "e-Filing" link.

Any person or the Commission's staff may, within 60 days after issuance of the instant notice by the Commission, file pursuant to Rule 214 of the Commission's Procedural Rules (18 CFR 855.214) a motion to intervene or notice of intervention and pursuant to Section 157.205 of the Regulations under the Natural Gas Act (18 CFR 157.205) a protest to the request. If no protest is filed within the time allowed, therefore, the proposed activity shall be deemed to be authorized effective the day after the time allowed for filing a protest. If a protest is filed and not withdrawn within 30 days after the time allowed for filing a protest, the instant request shall be treated as an application for authorization pursuant to Section 7 of the Natural Gas Act.

Comment Date: April 31, 2011

UNITED STATES OF AMERICA
BEFORE THE
FEDERAL ENERGY REGULATORY COMMISSION

North Central Gas Pipeline Company   Docket No. CP11-6666-000

REQUEST FOR BLANKET AUTHORIZATION

Pursuant to Sections 157.205 and 157.21 l(a)(2) of the regulations of the Federal Energy Regulatory Commission ("Commission"), 18 C.F.R. §§ 157.205 and 157.211(a)(2) (2005), North Central Gas Pipeline Company ("NORTH CENTRAL") hereby provides prior notice that it intends to construct, own and operate a delivery point to serve Fantastic Manufacturing Company ("Fantastic") located in Homersville, MN. The proposed service will bypass the local distribution service currently provided to Fantastic by the Town of Homersville ("Homersville'). Consistent with the Commission's regulations, NORTH CENTRAL will not commence activities associated with this project until all appropriate procedures, including the notice and comment period, have been completed. NORTH CENTRAL will comply with all applicable environmental regulations that apply to its proposed project, including those set forth in Section 157.206(b) of the Commission's regulations, 18 C.F.R. § 157.206(b) (2006).

I.

The exact legal name of NORTH CENTRAL is North Central Gas Pipeline Company. Correspondence and communications concerning this request should be directed are as follows:

Andre Gide	Al Smith
Vice President, Regulatory	General Counsel
North Central Gas Pipeline Company	North Central Gas Pipeline Company
Post Office Box 42000000000	Post Office Box 42000000000
Wonderfields, MN	Wonderfields, MN
Telephone: (666) 777-7777	Telephone: (666) 777-7777
Facsimile: (666) 777-7778	Facsimile: (666) 777-7778

II.

NORTH CENTRAL currently holds a blanket certificate under Subpart F of Part 157 of the Commission's regulations.

Pursuant to Section 157.211 (a)(2) of the Commission's regulations and its blanket certificate, NORTH CENTRAL seeks authority herein to construct, own and operate facilities necessary to deliver natural gas to serve Fantastic Manufacturing's manufacturing facilities in Homersville, MN. To establish this delivery point, NORTH CENTRAL proposes to install a 4-inch hot tap on its 16" pipeline at approximately milepost 127, and approximately 1.2 miles of 4-inch pipeline as a delivery lateral, plus an appropriate meter and appurtenant facilities. The delivery point will be located on Fantastic' property. The pipeline delivery lateral will extend across property owned by Homersville, MN, which currently serves Fantastic. A USGS topographic map showing the location of the proposed facilities is attached as Volume II. [VOLUME II IS OMITTED FROM PUBLIC MATERIALS FOR SECURITY REASONS.]

NORTH CENTRAL estimates the total cost of the proposed facilities to be approximately $900,000. Fantastic will reimburse NORTH CENTRAL for the costs associated with such facilities.

The new delivery point will be used by Fantastic to receive up to 5,000 Dth per day of natural gas from NORTH CENTRAL for utilization at its factory. Upon completion of the construction of the delivery point, NORTH CENTRAL will commence open-access transportation service to Fantastic in accordance with its filed tariff and Part 284 of the Commission's regulations.

Pursuant to Section 157.211(a)(2)(i) of the Commission's regulations, NORTH CENTRAL notes that the Town of Homersville is the local distribution company currently providing natural gas service to Fantastic. NORTH CENTRAL has complied with Section 284.13(f) of the Commission's regulations by providing written notification to Homersville and the Homersville Town Council. (Out of an abundance of caution, NORTH CENTRAL has also provided notice to the state public utility commission even though Homersville Gas is not regulated by such agency.)

IV.

The addition of this delivery point will not have a significant impact on NORTH CENTRAL's annual deliveries or peak day operations because gas service will be provided under NORTH CENTRAL's authorized level of service. NORTH CENTRAL has sufficient capacity to render the proposed service without detriment or disadvantage to services provided to its existing customers, and its tariff does not prohibit the installation of the proposed facilities.

NORTH CENTRAL believes that, apart from its consultation with the U.S. Fish and Wildlife Service and the Minnesota State Historical Office, no filing to supplement or effectuate the instant request must be or is to be filed by NORTH CENTRAL with any federal, state, or other regulatory body.

V.

In accordance with Section 157.206(b) of the Commission's regulations, NORTH CENTRAL has attached as Appendix 1 all environmental clearances required to construct the subject delivery point.[1] Appropriate notice will be given to landowners whose property will be affected by this proposal. NORTH CENTRAL has filed maps showing the exact location of the proposed facilities but has omitted such maps from

---

[1] North Central conducted a standard review of published literature concerning wildlife, habitat and historic sites in the potential construction area. Nothing was identified requiring further consultation with USFWS. The Minnesota SHPO concurred that no further investigation was needed of possible historic sites.

the public record for security reasons. Intervenors may view the maps at NORTH CENTRAL's offices during normal business hours.

VI.

Appended hereto is a statement in conformity with Section 157.205(b)(5) of the Commission's Regulations suitable for publication in the Federal Register, summarizing the instant request.

VII.

WHEREFORE, North Central Gas Pipeline Company respectfully requests that the Commission, after giving public notice of this filing, allow NORTH CENTRAL to construct, own and operate the delivery point and related facilities in order to deliver natural gas to Fantastic.

Respectfully submitted,
NORTH CENTRAL GAS PIPELINE COMPANY

By: _____

Andre Gide
Vice President, Regulatory Affairs
Dated: February 31, 2011

VERIFICATION

STATE OF MINNESOTA

COUNTY OF WINABAGO

} SS

    Andre Gide, being duly sworn upon his oath says: that he is Vice President, Regulatory Affairs at North Central Gas Pipeline Company, that he has read the foregoing "Request for Blanket Authorization" and has personal knowledge of the matters therein set forth; that the facts therein stated are true to the best of his knowledge, information, and belief; that the paper copy of the foregoing filing contains the same information on the accompanying diskette; and that the activities proposed in said Request comply with the requirements of Part 157, Subpart F of the Federal Energy Regulatory Commission's Regulations Under the Natural Gas Act.

SUBSCRIBED AND SWORN to before me this 31st day of February, 2011.

Notary Public
Sesame Street
Wonderfields, MN

(SEAL)

My commission expires:

Appendix 1

North Central Gas Pipeline Company (NCGP) Compliance with FERC Standard Environmental Conditions (18 CFR 157.206(b)) for Blanket and 311 Projects.

Project Name: Fantastic Interconnect

Location: Homersville, MN   AFE: _____

Prepared by: _____   Date:11/31/10

	157.206(b) No./Requirement	Assessment of Project Compliance (revise standard entries, as needed)
1	Construction according to 18 CFR 380.15	CFR 380.15 requirements are incorporated in NCGP's Construction Standards
2(i), 3(iv)	Clean Water Act and associated regulations (e.g., NPDES, Corps); comply w/FERC "Upland Erosion Control, Revegetation and Maintenance Plan" and Wetland and Water body Construction and Mitigation Procedures.	Exempt from NPDES permitting as an oil & gas facility. FERC Plans & Procedures compliance integrated into NCGP construction standards. No discharges planned.
2(ii)	Clean Water Act and associated regulations	Project will result in no change in air emission sources.
2(iii + iv) 3(ii)	Cultural Resources Clearance	SHPO MOU, dated 8/12/07, valid through 8/12/12.
2(vi), 3(i), 7	Endangered Species Clearance	USFWS MOU dated 11/31/07, valid through 11/31/12
2(vii)	Exec Order 11998: Floodplain Management	Project will not occur in a designated floodplain.
2(viii)	Exec. Order 11990: Protection of Wetlands	Project will comply with requirements for construction in wetlands.
2(ix)	Wild & Scenic Rivers Act	Project will not occur near a designated wild or scenic river.
2(x)	National Wilderness Act	Project will not occur within a designated national wilderness.
2(xi)	National Parks and Recreation Act of 1978	Project will not occur within a designated national park or recreation area.
2(xii)	Magnuson-Stevens Fisher Conservation and Management Act	Project will not occur within an area affected by Act jurisdiction

	157.206(b) No./Requirement	Assessment of Project Compliance (revise standard entries, as needed)
4	No significant adverse impact on sensitive environmental area	Project will occur within a park but will follow standard construction, restoration and maintenance requirements to mitigate impacts.
5	No project compressor facility noise above 55 dB(A) at NSAs	Project does not involve the installation of compressor horsepower.
6(i)	Proposed 157.208 facility > 0.5 mi. from existing or proposed and permitted Nuclear plant	Project will not occur within .5 miles of a nuclear power plant.
6(ii)	Proposed underground storage and testing project > 2 mi. from existing or proposed and permitted Nuclear plant	Project will not occur within 2 miles of a nuclear power plant

U.S. FISH AND WILDLIFE SERVICE

LETTER OF CONCURRENCE
MINOR PROJECTS IN MINNESOTA

In compliance with Federal Energy Regulatory Commission (FERC) Rule 234 authorizing the issuance of Certificates of Public Convenience and Necessity, North Central Gas Pipeline Company its subsidiaries and affiliates (Company), is required to obtain concurrence from the U.S. Fish and Wildlife Service (Service) that any proposed construction by the Company will not have adverse effects on listed or proposed species or their habitats as identified in the Endangered Species Act (ESA) of 1973, as amended (16 U.S.C. 1531 et. seq). This concurrence authorizes the Company determine that various low-impact projects will not adversely affect listed species and to conduct minor gas pipeline construction projects as defined below.

The primary areas of concern regarding construction projects are threatened and endangered species, species proposed for listing as threatened or endangered, raptors and migratory birds. The following habitat types should be avoided in order for this clearance to be in effect: raptor sites; prairie dog towns; wetlands; and designated Bald Eagle nesting areas. In the event of potential effects to any of these types of areas, the Service prefers to review and evaluate the proposal individually.

If the Company, as FERC's designated representative for these projects, determines that any proposed activity may affect a federally listed threatened or endangered species or its habitat, formal consultation should be initiated between FERC and the Service. If there will be no effect, or if the Service concurs in writing there will be beneficial effects, then further consultation is not necessary. A species list and range information is included herewith to assist the Company evaluate project sites for potential threatened and endangered species.

At least every year, the Company will contact the Service to determine whether updated listed species stews or updated range maps are needed.

If the Company's review indicates no potential effect to any of the above listed Service concerns, then this clearance letter allows the Company to complete the following very limited, low-impact project types without contacting the Service for review: the addition or removal of pipeline taps, meter settings, dehydrators, and cathodic protection equipment and groundbeds; any repair. replacement, abandonment or new pipelines of two miles or less; construction or enhancement of compressor or treating units and associated equipment on existing station properties; any monitoring facilities occupying less than three acres; any abandonments that require minor construction activities including removal of existing structures; and any activities not involving earth disturbance.

Proposed projects which involve construction other than those included above, those that impact the habitats of concern listed above, or projects determined to have a potential "may affect" would require site-specific review by the Service.

This letter of concurrence will be in effect for a period of five (5) years from the date it is signed by the Service. It may be modified with the approval of both the Service and the Company. Approval of any such modification will be indicated by written acceptance.

By: Andrew Andrews, Field Supervisor

Date November 31, 2008

UNITED STATES OF AMERICA
BEFORE THE
FEDERAL ENERGY REGULATORY COMMISSION

North Central Gas Pipeline Company   Docket No. CP11-6666-000

MOTION TO INTERVENE AND PROTEST OF
HOMERSVILLE AUDUBON SOCIETY

Pursuant to Rules 211 and 214 of the Federal Energy Regulatory Commission's ("Commission") Rules of Practice and Procedure,[2] Homersville Audubon Society ("HAS") hereby submits its Motion to Intervene and Protest regarding the certificate application by North Central Gas Pipeline Company ("North Central") to construct and operate a new pipeline lateral and delivery point to serve Fantastic Manufacturing Company ("Fantastic"). In support, HAS respectfully states the following:

I. MOTION TO INTERVENE

Communications concerning this motion should be addressed as follows, and the following should be included on the official service list in this proceeding:

Bob White BLACK AND WHITE 13000 Pennsylvania Avenue Homersville, MN 77777 (050) 399-0110 (phone) (050) 399-0111 (fax) bwhite@blackandwhitelaw.com(email)	Robin Nester President Homersville Audubon Society P.O. Box 90696 Homersville, MN (050) 399-4149 (phone) (050) 399-4148 (fax) (email)rnester@HAS.org

The Homersville Audubon Society is an association of bird watchers and nature enthusiasts who live in or near Homersville, MN. HAS has a membership of approximately 80 individuals. Members of HAS regularly utilize the Homersville Bird Sanctuary (Sanctuary) for bird watching and nature walks. Some members of HAS volunteer to lead small groups to observe birds, animals, flowers and trees located in the Sanctuary. Most members of HAS are residents of Homersville whose taxes help support the Sanctuary. Some members make charitable donations to help support the Sanctuary.

This case involves review of North Central's certificate application to construct and operate pipeline facilities running through the Homersville Bird Sanctuary. The Homersville Bird Sanctuary is a 500 acre mix of woodlands and meadow, which is owned and managed by the Town of Homersville. It is a major attraction for HAS members as well other residents in the Homersville area. If a certificate of public

---

[2] 18 C.F.R. §§ 385.211 and.214 (2010).

convenience and necessity is issued as requested by North Central, the Bird Sanctuary will be subject to eminent domain, tree removal, pipeline construction, harm to wildlife, and future limitations on public use of the Sanctuary.

The certificate application, if approved, will adversely affect HAS's members, the Homersville Bird Sanctuary and the birds and habitat therein, Consequently, HAS and its members may be affected by the outcome of this proceeding. HAS has a substantial and vital interest herein and desires to intervene in order to protect that interest. Therefore, HAS is an interested party within the meaning of Section 15(a) of the Natural Gas Act, and its intervention and participation will be in the public interest. HAS is not now, and will not be, adequately represented by any other party in this proceeding, and may be bound or adversely affected by the Commission's action herein.

In consideration of the foregoing, Homersville Audubon Society respectfully requests that the Commission permit it to intervene with full rights as a party hereto.

II. PROTEST AND REQUEST FOR EVIDENTIARY HEARINGS

The Commission should reject North Central's application as being contrary to the public convenience and necessity. At a minimum, it should undertake a proper consultation with the U.S. Fish and Wildlife Service (Department of Interior) pursuant to the Endangered Species Act (ESA), and prepare an environmental impact statement, as required by the National Environmental Policy Act (NEPA), and set the matter for an evidentiary hearing to resolve contested issues of material fact.

Under its proposal, North Central would construct pipeline through the heart of the Homersville Bird Sanctuary, a public nature park and bird sanctuary owned by the Town of Homersville, in order to take Homersville's largest customer. The proposed project would harm the environment, an endangered species and its habitat, and a public nature preserve, as well as members of HAS and other citizens who treasure the park and bird sanctuary.

HAS understands that the Commission has a long-standing policy in favor of allowing customers to choose their suppliers of natural gas transportation services, even in cases involving bypasses of the user's traditional supplier, such as Homersville. The Commission also has "blanket certificate" rules authorizing a variety of routine projects subject to standard notice, approval and construction conditions. However, this case is NOT a routine construction case. The numerous negative impacts to the environment and to HAS and its members greatly outweigh the presumed benefits to two entities (Fantastic and North Central) from the blanket certificate proposal.

First, unlike other cases decided by the Commission, the pipeline in this case would be constructed through the middle of a public nature park and bird sanctuary owned by Homersville. The Sanctuary would be permanently and severely harmed by North Central's proposed construction and its permanent 75-foot right of way through nearly one-half mile of trees and a half-mile wide meadow. The entire right of way would be permanently cleared of trees and significant shrubbery. The wooden walkway would be cut in two by the heavy construction equipment, though it could presumably be rebuilt.

Second, HAS members regularly use the Sanctuary, and their use and enjoyment of the sanctuary would be permanently and irreparably harmed both visually and physically. HAS members fear that populations of birds and animals, which they regularly see now, will be reduced. The visual enjoyment of the undisturbed Sanctuary will be marred with large gaps permanently cut through the trees. The silence they experience now will be displaced by roaring machines during the construction phase and who knows what kind of interference thereafter. As discussed below, the habitat of an endangered species and perhaps the species itself would be harmed by the construction and permanent changes to the local environment. The Commission must protect the public from North Central's despoiling the nature park and bird sanctuary. FERC's regulations discourage pipeline construction in Federal and State parks and preserves, and the same policy should apply to a sanctuary and park owned by a local government.

Third, as previously noted and as discussed in the attached affidavit, an endangered species of bird (William's Flycatcher) has been spotted by a number of HAS members over the last two years. The species is typically found in mature forests, occasionally flying into open meadows for insects — just the sort of habitat offered by the Homersville Bird Sanctuary. Some individuals (*at least* two males and one female) have been seen, on a number of occasions by many of HAS' members, in the area in which the pipeline will be built. Construction will damage the forest and meadow habitat of this endangered species. The Commission must reject North Central's proposal because of the project's harm to individuals and habitat of this endangered species.

Fourth, this project is inconsistent with the Endangered Species Act. In the Endangered Species Act, Congress declared its policy that "all Federal departments and agencies shall seek to conserve endangered species and threatened species and shall utilize their authorities in furtherance of the purposes of this chapter." Section 2 of ESA, 16 U.S.C. 1531. It also required Federal agencies such as FERC to consult with the Secretary of Interior (which is undertaken through the U.S. Fish and Wildlife Service) concerning potential adverse impacts and mitigation. Section 7 of ESA, 16 U.S.C. 1536.

Not only will North Central's proposal unnecessarily harm an endangered species and its habitat, but FERC has not complied with the statutory requirement to evaluate impacts and consult with the Department of Interior based on the best scientific data available. Neither North Central nor this Commission has adequately consulted with the U.S. Fish and Wildlife Service (USFWS) concerning endangered species and habitat that may be affected by the proposed project. This duty to consult belongs to the agency. FERC cannot duck its obligation by appointing the self-interested pipeline company as its "non-Federal representative" for consultation and then looking the other way. Nor can the endangered species review be left to a simple search of published literature, which, in this case, was out of date. At a minimum, the Commission must conduct appropriate surveys and high-level consultations with USFWS concerning potential harms and whether mitigation is possible. The public interest in preserving William's Flycatcher is too important to be ignored, and it outweighs any arguable public or private interest to be obtained from the proposed bypass.

Fifth, the Commission is required by NEPA to prepare an environmental impact statement, which fully analyzes both the environmental impacts from the proposed project and the alternatives thereto. One obvious alternative is "no action" (*i.e.*, not to build a new pipeline) since Fantastic can continue to get natural gas from Homersville. Even if it were to serve Fantastic, North Central could find a route that goes outside the Sanctuary. With a full record of the proposed pipeline's harms and the available alternatives, FERC would correctly conclude that the proposal does not serve the public convenience and necessity.

Sixth, just because North Central wants to save money by going through the Sanctuary does not mean that such destruction of a public preserve is justified. It is inevitably cheaper to take park land than to take private land, which would cost more. If cheapness were the only measure, then all of the nation's parks and refuges would be crossed by roads, pipelines, electric lines, etc. It is the duty of this Federal agency to protect the public interest from such harms. Compensation for a taking of park or sanctuary land will never compensate the public for a loss of precious resources such as the Homersville Bird Sanctuary.

CONCLUSION

In conclusion, the Commission should grant HAS' motion to intervene and summarily reject or order rerouting of the project or, at least, conduct a thorough review of the harms it would do, including conducting a NEPA review, a proper consultation with U.S.F.W.S., and a full evidentiary hearing in which all contested issues of material fact can be resolved on a fair record.

Respectfully submitted

_____

Bob White
BLACK AND WHITE
13000 Pennsylvania Avenue
Homersville, MN 77777
(050) 399-0110 (phone)
(050) 399-0111 (fax)
bwhite@blackandwhitelaw.com(email)

AFFIDAVIT OF ROBIN NESTER, PHD

My name is Robin Nester. I am the President of the Homersville Audubon Society. I am also a resident of Homersville, where I have lived for 8 years.

1. I have an undergraduate degree in biology and ecology. I have a Ph.D in biology from Northernmost University, where my studies emphasized ornithology. I currently teach biology and ornithology at Homersville College.

2. I regularly visit the Homersville Bird Sanctuary where I often lead bird-watching trips for my college students and for groups of amateur birdwatchers.

3. On several occasions during the past year, I have had the good fortune of spotting William's Flycatcher. I have seen at least two males and one female at various times. They were located near where I understand North Central's construction will go. (The fact that North Central has refused to make the exact route public makes it difficult to be sure where it will go, but I have a pretty good idea.) I spotted one male and one female together during the Spring of this year. I cannot tell if there has been any nesting activity, but the timing makes it possible.

4. My students and several members of HAS have told me that they saw William's Flycatcher on at least three other occasions.

5. We have discussed these sightings at HAS meetings. By phone, I have alerted Homersville's park Superintendant and a US Fish and Wildlife official to the sightings. Although I am preparing a paper, I have not yet published my findings. I am afraid that publicizing the location of an endangered species might attract malicious individuals who might disturb the birds.

6. I am only making a more public statement now in order to protect the birds and their habitat from the harm that would occur if North Central were to construct the pipeline which it proposes in this case.

7. In my opinion, the proposal should be rejected as being too dangerous to the habitat and survival of William's Flycatcher. These birds depend primarily for nesting and feeding habitat upon forest of the type found at the Homersville Bird Sanctuary. They also can be seen flying into meadows adjacent to such forests, such as one finds in the Homersville Bird Sanctuary. The proposed clearing and the construction and the on-going maintenance of a pipeline in those areas are likely to harm the survival of William's Flycatcher in this part of the country. The risk of harm will be particularly great if these individuals are, in fact, nesting in the area.

Robin Nester, PhD
Subscribed and sworn before me this 1st day of April, 2011.
Notary Public
[certificate of service-omitted]

SUMMARY OF OTHER PROTESTS

Town of Homersville — You are writing it.

International Birders Union — IBU states its strong opposition to construction of a pipeline through the sanctuary and any actions that might harm Williams Flycatcher or its habitat. It incorporates the Homersville Audubon Society's protests and Dr. Robin Nester's affidavit by reference.

Homersville Taxpayers Alliance — HTA estimates that more than $12,000,000 have been spent on the bird sanctuary in the last 20 years. That money came from taxpayers like HTA's members. HTA's members would lose the value of their investment in the sanctuary and would lose some of the benefits of the park for which they have been forced to pay all these years. The loss of Fantastic as a customer will also hurt HTAs members, who will end up bearing those costs through higher gas rates or higher taxes. Homersville isn't going to get the money from anywhere else.

Mid-Central Pipeline Company — Mid-Central is a competing interstate natural gas pipeline. It is fully capable of serving Fantastic without any need to construct through the Homersville Bird Sanctuary. Consistent with the Commission's stated policy preference, Mid-Central could construct its pipeline to Fantastic entirely along existing, disturbed rights of way and would completely avoid construction in the Homersville Bird Sanctuary. The public interest in protecting sensitive environmental assets and wildlife strongly favors Mid-Central's pipeline. Also, Mid-Central asserts that when faced with competing projects, the Commission is obligated by *Ashbacker Radio Corp. v. FCC*, 326 U.S. 327 (1946) to conduct comparative hearings to enable the Commission to make an informed judgment concerning the overall public interest. Mid-Central requests such a hearing.